Scary, Gross, and Enlightening Books for Boys Grades 3-12

Deborah B. Ford

A Linworth Publishing Book

028.55 FOR
Ford, Deborah B.
Scary, gross, and enlightening:
books for boys grades 3-12 /

Libraries Unlimited
An Imprint of ABC-CLIO, LLC

A B C 🟆 C L I O

Santa Barbara, California • Denver, Colorado • Oxford, England

Copyright © 2010 by Libraries Unlimited

Library of Congress Cataloging-in-Publication Data

Ford, Deborah B.
  Scary, gross, and enlightening books for boys grades 3-12 / Deborah B. Ford.
    p. cm.
  Includes bibliographical references and index.
  ISBN 978-1-58683-344-2 (pbk.)
  1. Boys—Books and reading. 2. Reading promotion. I. Title.
  Z1039.B67F67   2010
  028.5'5—dc22   2009016877

14 13 12 11 10   1 2 3 4 5

This book is also available on the World Wide Web as an eBook.
Visit www.abc-clio.com for details.

ABC-CLIO, LLC
130 Cremona Drive, P.O. Box 1911
Santa Barbara, California 93116-1911

This book is printed on acid-free paper ∞
Manufactured in the United States of America

Table of Contents

Introduction

Whether your students are girls or boys, reading is an essential skill that will take them far in life. No longer is the GED as acceptable as a high school diploma. Simply put, employers would rather hire someone who has proven that they not only have the knowledge to be a good employee, but that they were able to complete a task.

National studies show that boys read an average of 1.5 grades behind girls. Boys ages 5 to 12 are 60% more likely to have repeated a grade. Fourth grade girls score 12% higher on writing tests than boys. Boys are 33% more likely to drop out of high school than girls. In essence, these studies show that boys are biologically, developmentally, and psychologically different than girls (Smith and Wilhelm, 2002). It's up to us as educators to turn those statistics around.

Scary, Gross, and Enlightening: Books for Boys Grades 3-12 will give you ideas to encourage your boys to read while teaching the same curriculum standards by giving you strategies and booklists that you can use in every subject, both in the classroom and school library.

The Books

All the rage now, books for boys have come to be known as anything that is gross or scary. In my experience, I have found that though boys do love books about body functions and horror, there are many other books that they will like if they are introduced to them. Look at what Rowling's series has done for readers of all ages! The number of pages in a book is less a factor than it was ten years ago. Publishers are now aware that boys choose books differently than girls, so they are encouraging authors to write for that audience. The choices are more bountiful. Walk through a bookstore and you can immediately spot a "boy book." Snakes, bugs, and underwear fill the shelves of bookstores. I have included many of these favorites in the chapter bibliographies.

However, as I prepared for this project, I also chose books that matched national curriculum standards. I read books that have won awards from the American Library Association. I looked for award winning books from the National Council for Social Studies and the National Science Teachers Association Notable lists. I looked for books that have great pictures, break out text boxes, and books with high interest-low vocabulary. I looked for books that have strong male main characters.

Many of these books will sell after reading the first sentence. Reading "If your teacher has to die, August isn't a bad time of year for it" (Richard Peck, *A Teacher's Funeral*) is a good example. On the other hand, some of the books in this manual may be what we call a "hand sell." Boys may not necessarily choose them unless their attention has been directed to the book. As a classroom teacher, teacher librarian, or public librarian, I hope you will make the time to market some of these books for your students or patrons.

I have also included the publisher's interest level recommendation {IL} and a reading level (an average of three standard tools) {RL} for each recommended book. However, remember that you are the expert who knows your students and community. You be the judge about whether a particular book works for your situation.

Strategies

This book provides you with lists of books that boys and other readers will enjoy, but there are some other keys to success that we must remember. For example, students need choices. Allow your students or patrons to choose what they want to read and re-select if they make a less than perfect choice. Books are like shoes; every shoe doesn't fit every foot.

We must keep our target audience in mind as we make selections for reading choices. If every book is a "girl" book, then we potentially turn off a good portion of our readers. If we are to dispel the myth that reading is for girls, we must show students that it is for everyone. For some of us, that means that we will have to loosen up a little bit. Some of the suggested books are not what we might call "great literature." However, they will get kids to read. After awhile, kids will move on to other titles. If we frown on their choices, we send a message that can be self-defeating. By allowing choice, we give them roots to spread their wings.

In each chapter, you will find Teacher/Librarian generic strategies for that particular genre. These strategies can be used by either the media specialist or classroom teacher. From time to time you will see specific ideas about specific books. I call them Blinding Flashes of Brilliance, marked with a genius bulb. The chapters are divided by genre, using ideas from boys (those who like to read and those who say they don't) and other reluctant readers. Some books are suggested in more than one chapter. Websites to support the activities or genre appear at the end of each chapter. Because websites often change, I have created a website to support this book <http://www.kn.att. com/wired/fil/pages/listboysandau.html>, which includes a link to my blog <http://www.deborahford.blogspot.com> that will update you on what I am currently reading. As new sites are discovered they will be added to this site.

Reading promotion activities and other non-traditional activities can also lead to an increase in the literacy of boys. Each chapter includes related programming ideas for the school and public library. Many of these may also be adapted for classroom situations.

The Challenge

In the years that students are in grades 3 to 12, boys especially, are at risk. In 1996 the U.S. Department of Education reported that male eleventh grade students scored at the same level as female students in the eighth grade (Taliaferro, 2001). In 2005 they determined that boys are 50% more likely to have failed a grade during elementary school. 80% of high school dropouts are male (Gurian, 2005). Awareness can be a key that unlocks many closed doors. By focusing on the differences between how boys and girls learn and how they develop reading and writing skills, we can be one step closer to making an impact in the lives of the students that we teach. By keeping learning styles in mind, developing strategies, and providing materials that will enable and encourage students to succeed, we may be able to make a difference in the lives of all students that we teach. Whether you are a classroom teacher, librarian, or even a parent, this book is designed to help you focus on the differences between boys and girls and meet the challenge of making all readers more successful.

Websites

Scary, Gross, and Enlightening: Books for Boys
<http://www.kn.att.com/wired/fil/pages/listboysandau.html>

Deborah Ford Libraries Matter Blog
<http://www.deborahford.blogspot.com>

20 Ways to Grow a Reader

1. Allow the reader to have a choice.

2. Provide comfortable reading areas.

3. Provide uninterrupted reading time.

4. Provide a variety of reading materials.

5. Read aloud.

6. Introduce readers to authors and illustrators.

7. Model reading; discuss what you are reading at home.

8. Regularly visit the library—both school *and* public.

9. Don't make them finish *every* book. Not all books fit every reader.

10. Ownership is important. Create or buy bookplates for kids to put in their own books.

11. Reading is its own reward.

12. Use booklists (nancykeane.com or databases like What Do I Read Next? Or NoveList for ideas).

13. Don't worry about making the reader choose "good books."

14. Write—anything, everything. Readers write and writers read.

15. Allow re-reading of favorite books.

16. Read the book *before* seeing the movie.

17. Play board games.

18. Follow cookbooks to create meals.

19. Use travel books to plan vacations.

20. Don't give up. Everyone has spurts of "non-reading."

Figure 1

CHAPTER 1

Just the Facts: Nonfiction

I f you lined up your elementary grade students who checked out books in the library in a physical graph by call number, most school librarians would tell you that the majority of students would fall into the 500s. They love to read about bugs, snakes, dinosaurs, and sharks. Facts, Just the Facts! More than 50% of the school library print collection is nonfiction. Textbooks are made of nonfiction, but many of our students read at a lower level, making those heavy tomes not only cumbersome in weight, but also in value. Adding nonfiction trade books and series not only provides the support material you need to meet your curriculum standards, they will sell like hotcakes!

Many books are successful because they are written in a series. With a series, students can rely on the same format with a well-designed appearance. What works with one subject in a series generally works with another topic. Series come in a variety of reading levels. There are many high interest-low vocabulary series for upper grade students, such as the Edge and Blazer books from Capstone Press Publishers. The series book can also take a dry topic and jazz it up. Look at the success of the DK Eyewitness books, for example.

Trade books that stand alone are also a mainstay of newer nonfiction. Many of these books utilize a magazine-like format. There are sidebars with relevant information. Pictures have clear captions. They have indexes, glossaries, and bold headings to assist the student in navigating through the material. However, most books for grades 3-8 are 112 pages or less. We should be careful when creating assignments for our students. Perhaps they could read several books on the same topic, allowing them to compare information.

National Geographic has excellent stand-alone and series titles that will support your curriculum standards. Several authors have distinguished themselves in this genre. Marc Aronson, Russell Freedman, Kathleen Krull, and Lynn Curle are just a few of the many authors who write exciting nonfiction books that your students may enjoy. Steering students towards these authors, publishers, or series will help provide them with the curriculum support they need and books that they will finish.

Using nonfiction books to support your content areas will assist students in locating facts, summarizing ideas, and reinforcing or reviewing curriculum standards. This chapter is aligned with the Dewey Decimal System. All bibliographies are sorted by their division and then by title. Books on sports and books on war or history are also located in their own chapters.

Teacher/Librarian Strategies:

- Have students write five facts from their nonfiction book. Have them compare those facts with information in another book or their textbook. A graphic organizer, such as a T-chart, may help them record their information.

- Classroom teachers can isolate nonfiction books from fiction in their classrooms, evaluating the number of books available while making it easier for students to find what they want.

- Classroom teachers should also adopt the school's collection development policy in their classrooms. Outdated, incorrect materials should be deleted from the classroom library. It's better to have no information than misinformation.

- In an elementary school, librarians can use shelf props or shelf markers to quickly identify nonfiction sections. For example, place a bean bag fish near the fish books or a baseball glove near the books about baseball. In middle or high school, students can create

Shelf Links—signs that give a call number and a graphic to notate the subject. This is especially helpful to students whose second language is English.

- Many times teachers require students to choose a book that exceeds a particular number of pages. In today's world of literature, most books for grades 3-8 are well under 100 pages. If they are over 100 pages, they tend to be a higher reading level and are more suited for grades 9-12. If you are concerned about length, ask students to read more than one book on the subject.

- Have students evaluate the information in the nonfiction work: How clear are the photographs? Is it indexed? Is there a glossary? Students can then rate their books.

- Allow students to write blurbs about their favorite series or nonfiction book and place them with the book in the Student Picks section of the school library or on the library website.

- Host a storytelling festival after students have chosen nonfiction books for the telling.

Nonfiction Books

General Works and Philosophy 000-100s

Title — Author. {Interest Level, Dewey Decimal Classification} — Publisher, Year, Reading Level, Number of Pages

---

The dangerous book for boys — Iggulden, Conn. {IL 5-8, 031} — Collins, 2007, RL 5.9, 270p

A collection of entertainments geared toward boys, containing accounts of famous battles, William Shakespeare quotations, games, and instructions for activities such as building a go-cart, cutting flint heads, making an electromagnet, and folding the "greatest paper airplane in the world."

Dear author: letters of hope — {IL YA, 028.5} — Philomel Books, 2007, RL 7.0, 222p

Offers a collection of letters from students to an assortment of authors about the impact of their work on the lives of their readers, accompanied by the author's responses.

Encyclopedia horrifica: the terrifying truth! about vampires, ghosts, monsters, and more — Gee, Joshua. {IL 3-6, 001.9} — Scholastic, 2007, RL 6.6, 129p

A collection of interviews, rare images, and eyewitness accounts of paranormal and unexplained phenomena, with topics ranging from UFOs to psychic activity and sea monsters.

Even more children's miscellany: smart, silly, and strange information that's essential to know — Macdonald, Guy. {IL 3-6, 031.02} — Chronicle Books, 2008, 2006, RL 6.9, 126p

Contains an eclectic array of facts, chronologies, and lists ranging from history, astronomy, and biology to games, world records, and other miscellaneous information.

For boys only: the biggest, baddest book ever — Aronson, Marc. {IL 5-8, 031.02} — Feiwel and Friends, 2007, RL 6, 157p

A compendium of information on a variety of topics of interest to boys, such as how to fight off an alligator, make fake blood, escape from being tied-up, land an airplane, and much more.

Guinness World Records, 2008 — {IL YA, 031} — Bantam Books, 2008, RL 7.0, 613p

Presents the biggest, smallest, fastest, longest, and other world records in such categories as the human body, human achievement, life on Earth, engineering, science and technology, arts and media, and sports and games.

> Books like *Guinness* will stay checked out if you let them go out of the library. Why not buy extra copies and mark them "For Library Use Only." It's a great kid magnet!

Kidchat gone wild!: 202 creative questions to unleash the imagination — Nicholaus, Bret. {IL 3-6, 031.02} — Roaring Brook Press, 2007, RL 4.4, unpaged

A collection of 202 questions based on imaginative possibilities and designed to encourage family discussions and help parents and children get to know one another better.

Mysteries unwrapped: mutants & monsters — Ho, Oliver. {IL 3-6, 001.944} — Sterling, 2008, RL 5.9, 88p

> Describes legendary monsters, such as Bigfoot, Nessie, and the kraken; and includes anecdotes about alleged sightings.

The ultimate teen book guide — {IL YA, 028.1} — Walker & Co., 2008, 432p

> Teen reviewers and popular authors offer recommendations for more than seven hundred books from all genres, including classics, cult fiction, award winners, bestsellers, fantasy, and graphic novels.

The world almanac for kids 2008 — {IL 3-6, 031.02} — World Almanac Books, Distributed to the trade in the United States by Simon and Schuster, 2007, RL 8.6, 352p

> Provides information on topics of particular interest to kids, such as United States history, art, weather, music, and sports; and features fun facts, puzzles, games, activities, jokes, maps, flags, source websites, and photographs.

Religion 200s

Title — Author. {Interest Level, Dewey Decimal Classification} — Publisher, Year, Reading Level, Number of Pages

Do hard things: a teenage rebellion against low expectations — Harris, Alex. {IL YA, 248.8} — Multnomah Books, 2008, 241p

> Nineteen-year-old twins Alex and Brett Harris challenge teenagers to reject the "low expectations" of contemporary culture and "do hard things" for God, discussing the Bible and five ways to transform oneself and work for social change.

Mythological creatures: a classical bestiary: tales of strange beings, fabulous creatures, fearsome beasts, & hideous monsters from Ancient Greek mythology — Curlee, Lynn. {IL 3-6, 292.2} — Atheneum Books for Young Readers, 2008, RL 6.8, 35p

> An illustrated guide to the beasts often found in ancient myths that describes each creature's origins and what role it has played in world mythology.

Social Sciences, Folklore 300s

Title — Author. {Interest Level, Dewey Decimal Classification} — Publisher, Year, Reading Level, Number of Pages

---

As good as anybody: Martin Luther King Jr. and Abraham Joshua Heschel's amazing march towards freedom — Michelson, Richard. {IL 3-6, 323} — Alfred A. Knopf, 2008, RL 3.2, 38p

Describes the experiences that influenced Martin Luther King Jr., and Abraham Joshua Heschels's civil rights activism and discusses the friendship between the two men.

Bearskinner: a tale of the Brothers Grimm — Schlitz, Laura Amy. {IL 3-6, 398.2} — Candlewick Press, 2007, RL 4, 30p

A retelling of the Grimm fairy tale in which a despondent soldier makes a pact to do the devil's bidding for seven years in return for as much money and property as he could ever want.

Beowulf: a hero's tale retold — Rumford, James. {IL 5-8, 398.2} — Houghton Mifflin, 2007, RL 4.2, 48p

A simplified and illustrated retelling of the exploits of the Anglo-Saxon warrior, Beowulf, and how he came to defeat the monster Grendel, Grendel's mother, and a dragon that threatened the kingdom.

Flush!: the scoop on poop throughout the ages — Harper, Charise Mericle. {IL K-3, 392.3} — Little, Brown, 2007, RL 3.8, 25p

Illustrations and rhyming text describe the history of toilets and the disposal of human waste.

An inconvenient truth: the crisis of global warming — Gore, Albert. {IL YA, 363.738} — Viking, Rodale, 2007, RL 7.4, 191p

An adaptation of the book in which former Vice President Al Gore examines the climate crisis that is threatening the future of the planet, describes what the world's governments are doing to correct the problem, and explains why the problem should be taken more seriously.

Little Rooster's diamond button — MacDonald, Margaret Read. {IL K-3, 398.2} — Albert Whitman, 2007, RL 2.4, 32p

Little Rooster is happy to find a diamond button—it's a perfect present for his mistress. Then the king snatches the button for his treasure chamber. When Little Rooster demands the button back, the king has him thrown into a well.

Mysteries of the mummy kids — Halls, Kelly Milner. {IL 5-8, 393} — Darby Creek Pub., 2007, RL 7.8, 72p

Explores mummies from around the world, focusing on mummified children; and provides information about their deaths, the sites where they were found, and what caused their preservation.

Race: a history beyond black and white — Aronson, Marc. {IL YA, 394.2663} — Ginee Seo Books/Atheneum Books for Young Readers, 2007, RL 8.8, 322p

Marc Aronson traces the history of racial prejudice in the Western world from ancient times to the present, identifying events and individuals that have influenced people's conceptions about race.

The real story of stone soup — Compestine, Ying Chang. {IL K-3, 398.2} — Dutton Children's Books, 2007, RL 2.9, 30p

When a crew of Chinese fishermen forget to bring cooking utensils with them, they find creative ways to make do with what they have and what they can find.

> How many versions of Stone Soup do you have? Make a game of the Old Venn and see who can come up with the most unique answers.

Rest in peace: a history of American cemeteries — Greene, Meg. {IL 5-8, 393.09} — Twenty-First Century Books, 2008, RL 7.4, 112p

Chronicles the history of American cemeteries from prehistoric times through 2005, looking at how burial traditions and rituals have changed, and discussing trends enabled by technology.

The ultimate weapon: the race to develop the atomic bomb — Sullivan, Edward T. {IL YA, 355.8} — Holiday House, 2007, RL 9.5, 182p

Chronicles the three-year Manhattan Project, discussing scientific developments, scientists, the three secret cities, spies, and saboteurs; and describes the decision to use the atom bomb on Japan, the dropping of the bombs, and the aftermath.

> Some award winners may need a "hand-sell" to get kids to read them. <u>Some nonfiction books</u> may be one of them. Share a bit and watch it fly!

We are one: the story of Bayard Rustin — Brimner, Larry Dane. {IL 3-6, 323} — Calkins Creek, 2007, RL 6.3, 48p

Chronicles the life of African-American social activist Bayard Rustin, discussing his protests of segregation before the civil rights movement began and his organization of the March on Washington.

What's the big idea?: four centuries of innovation in Boston — Krensky, Stephen. {IL 3-6, 330.9774} — Charlesbridge, Boston History & Innovation Collaborative, 2008, RL 4.7, 64p

Historical photographs, illustrations, and easy-to-follow text introduce students to the people, inventions, and events from Boston that have influenced human history.

Language 400s

Title — Author. {Interest Level, Dewey Decimal Classification} — Publisher, Year, Reading Level, Number of Pages

---

L is for lollygag: quirky words for a clever tongue — {IL 5-8, 428.1} — Chronicle Books, 2008, RL 8, 125p

Contains alphabetically arranged entries that provide definitions of quirky words, each with a pronunciation guide.

Natural Science (Animals, Nature) 500s

Title — Author. {Interest Level, Dewey Decimal Classification} — Publisher, Year, Reading Level, Number of Pages

---

> Look carefully at your 500s library collection. Black and white photos or illustrations? Correct or not, kids won't read them. Buy new editions for that real estate.

Bodies from the ice — Deem, James. {IL 5-8, 550} — Houghton Mifflin, 2008, RL 8.3, 58p

> Examines the science of glaciers and looks at some of the discoveries of the past that have been made as the ice masses move and melt, including the preserved frozen remains of Otzi, the oldest human mummy ever found in ice, believed to be at least 5,300 years old.

Boy, were we wrong about the solar system! — Kudlinski, Kathleen V. {IL K-3, 523.2} — Dutton Children's Books, 2008, RL 4, 32p

> Looks at scientific discovery as a process of mistakes, mishaps, and enlightenment, and discusses how theories have changed throughout the history of research into the solar system.

The day the world exploded: the earthshaking catastrophe at Krakatoa — Zimmerman, Dwight Jon. {IL 5-8, 551.21} — Collins, 2008, RL 8.4, 96p

> Presents an illustrated account of the volcano eruption on the island of Krakatoa on August 27, 1883, and its aftermath.

Dino-dinners — Manning, Mick. {IL K-3, 567.9} — Holiday House, 2007, RL 2.7, 28p

> Illustrations and simple text describe the eating habits of various dinosaurs.

Dinosaur eggs discovered!: unscrambling the clues — Dingus, Lowell. {IL 5-8, 567.90982} — Twenty-First Century Books, 2008, RL 8.9, 112p

> Provides interesting facts and information on dinosaur eggs discovered in Patagonia by paleontologist Dr. Lowell Dingus.

> Heinemann Raintree Publishers has a Weed of the Month newsletter that will help you decide which books need to be weeded from your classroom or school library. Sign up online at their website.

The discovery and mystery of a dinosaur named Jane — Williams, Judith. {IL 3-6, 567.912} — Enslow Publishers, 2008, RL 5.2, 48p

> Tells the story of the tyrannosaur Jane, from her discovery and excavation in the badlands of Montana to her display at the Burpee Museum in Rockford, Illinois, and explores the mysteries of her life millions of years ago.

Face to face with grizzlies — Sartore, Joel. {IL 3-6, 599.784} — National Geographic, 2007, RL 6.1, 32p

> Joel Sartore describes his experiences with bears while on assignment for *National Geographic* magazine, and provides basic information about bears' bodies, habitats, and behavior, as well as environmental and human factors that endanger bears. *(From Face to face series from National Geographic; new titles are yet to come)*

Foolish physics — Townsend, John. {IL 5-8, 530.09} — Raintree, 2007, RL 6, 56p

> Chronicles the history of physics, focusing on some of the stranger tales of eccentric scientists and dangerous experiments that led to discoveries and breakthroughs in the field.

Hide and seek: nature's best vanishing acts — Helman, Andrea. {IL K-3, 591.47} — Walker, 2008, RL 3.4, 40p

> Full-color, illustrated photographs describe a number of animals that are able to use camouflage in order to avoid danger.

How many ways can you catch a fly? — Jenkins, Steve. {IL K-3, 590} — Houghton Mifflin, 2008, RL 6.3, unpaged

> Looks at how different animals, such as a rainbow trout, chimney swift, and slender loris, approach the challenge of catching flies.

How we know what we know about our changing climate: scientists and kids explore global warming — Cherry, Lynne. {IL 5-8, 551.6} — Dawn Publications, 2008, RL 7.4, 66p

> Describes how and where scientists find evidence of climate change, including bird migration patterns, checking tree rings, and collecting mud cores; and offers advice to students on how to make a positive impact on the environment.

I wonder why there's a hole in the sky and other questions about the environment — Callery, Sean. {IL 3-6, 363.7} — Kingfisher, 2008, RL 5.8, 32p

> Examines various environmental issues, answers questions for children, and describes why there is life on Earth; discusses the ozone, pollution, improving homes to become more environmentally friendly, and other related topics.

Living color — Jenkins, Steve. {IL 3-6, 591.47} — Houghton Mifflin, 2007, RL 5.8, 32p

> Looks at a wide range of colorful animals, describing how their feathers, scales, shells, and skin help them survive, warn predators, signal friends, attract a mate, or hide from their enemies.

Look behind!: tales of animal ends — Schaefer, Lola M. {IL K-3, 590} — Greenwillow Books, 2008, RL 4.7, 32p

> Looks at the characteristics of different animal butts and how their owners use them, featuring one rear end for each letter in the alphabet.

Manfish: a story of Jacques Cousteau — Berne, Jennifer. {IL K-3, 551.46} — Chronicle Books, 2008, RL 3.9, 34p

> An illustrated biography of Jacques Cousteau, discussing how his youthful fascinations with filming and underwater exploration translated into his life's work, and telling of his later devotion to saving the ocean environment.

The mysterious universe: supernovae, dark energy, and black holes — Jackson, Ellen B. {IL 5-8, 523.8} — Houghton Mifflin, 2008, RL 7.5, 60p

> Contains an illustrated discussion of space phenomena such as supernovae, black holes, and dark energy, which scientists such as Dr. Alex Fillippenka and his High-Z Supernova Search Team believe is pushing the universe apart at an accelerating rate.

Neandertals: a prehistoric puzzle — La Pierre, Yvette. {IL YA, 569.9} — Twenty-First Century Books, 2008, RL 8.7, 112p

> Examines recent discoveries and DNA technology used in reevaluating archaeological evidence about Neandertals.

Nic Bishop frogs — Bishop, Nic. {IL K-3, 597.8} — Scholastic, 2008, RL 3.7, 48p

> Full-color, illustrated photographs describing the characteristics and behaviors of a variety of frogs around the world.

Nic Bishop spiders — Bishop, Nic. {IL K-3, 595.4} — Scholastic Nonfiction, 2007, RL 3.3, 48p

> Photographs and text provide basic information about various kinds of spiders.

Owen & Mzee: the language of friendship — Hatkoff, Isabella. {IL 3-6, 599.63} — Scholastic Press, 2007, RL 6, 34p

Text and color photos tell the true story of the friendship that developed at a Kenyan wildlife sanctuary between Owen, a baby hippopotamus orphaned by the 2004 Southeast Asian tsunami, and Mzee, a 130-year-old giant tortoise.

Pale Male: citizen hawk of New York City — Schulman, Janet. {IL 3-6, 598.9} — Knopf, 2008, RL 5.2, 34p

Recounts the true story of Pale Male, a red-tailed hawk living in New York City who has become one of the city's most-watched celebrities. Bird watchers, tourists, and residents admire the bird and his nest, built on a Fifth Avenue apartment building.

Predators — Seidensticker, John. {IL 3-6, 591.5} — Simon & Schuster Books for Young Readers, 2008, RL 6.6, 64p

Explores the characteristics of many different kinds of predators, from snakes to birds to big cats to carnivorous plants, discussing their natural weapons, killing strategies, and habitats; and profiles six major predators.

Science warriors: the battle against invasive species — Collard, Sneed. {IL 5-8, 590} — Houghton Mifflin, 2008, RL 7.6, 48p

Explains what invasive species are and the damage they cause to local economies and ecosystems, and looks at how scientists are working to combat these encroaching organisms. *(From the series, Scientists in the Field)*

Sisters & brothers: sibling relationships in the animal world — Jenkins, Steve. {IL K-3, 591.56} — Houghton Mifflin, 2008, RL 3.2, 32p

An illustrated picture book that investigates sibling relationships within the animal kingdom.

SuperCroc: Paul Sereno's dinosaur eater — Sereno, Paul C. {IL 3-6, 567.9} — Bearport Pub., 2007, RL 4.9, 32p

Follows paleontologist Paul Sereno as he unearths the fossil remains of a giant crocodile in the African country of Niger; and contains facts about how this giant animal lived during prehistoric times.

The tale of Pale Male: a true story — Winter, Jeanette. {IL K-3, 598.9} — Harcourt, 2007, RL 3, 32p

Tells the true story of two red-tailed hawks, Pale Male and Lola, who made their home atop an apartment building in New York City and sparked a protest by those who loved them when the apartment board had their eight-foot-wide nest cleared away.

Tracking trash: flotsam, jetsam, and the science of ocean motion — Burns, Loree Griffin. {IL 5-8, 551.46} — Houghton Mifflin, 2007, RL 7.3, 56p

Describes the work of a man who tracks trash as it travels great distances by way of ocean currents. *(From the Scientists in the Field series.)*

> Pre-reading idea for Scientists in the Field series:
>
> Anticipation Guide
> Before students read one of the Scientist in the Field series, have students generate a reason for reading. Students then read the book, giving an example to support or reject their answers with facts from the book.
>
> 1. Scientists ask a lot of questions.
> 2. Scientists sit at a table all day.
> 3. Scientists mostly do experiments.
> 4. Scientists mostly work on their own.

The wolves are back — George, Jean Craighead. {IL K-3, 599.773} — Dutton Children's Books, 2008, RL 2.5, 32p

Describes the ecological benefits brought about by the reintroduction of wolves into Yellowstone National Park.

Pure Science (Space, Human Body, Vehicles) 600s

Title — Author. {Interest Level, Dewey Decimal Classification} — Publisher, Year, Reading Level, Number of Pages

Belly-busting worm invasions!: parasites that love your insides! — Tilden, Thomasine E. Lewis. {IL 5-8, 616.3} — F. Watts, 2008, RL 5.5, 64p

Examines how various parasites can invade the body and create a number of problems, and describes methods of diagnosis, treatment, and prevention.

Circulating life: blood transfusion from ancient superstition to modern medicine — Winner, Cherie. {IL 5-8, 615} — Twenty-First Century Books, 2007, RL 8.2, 112p

Traces the history of blood transfusions, discussing how the transfer of blood from one person to another has been viewed and attempted from ancient times to the present, and examines common myths, superstitions, and practices surrounding their use.

Disgusting foods — Miller, Connie Colwell. {IL 5-8, 641.3} — Capstone Press, 2007, RL 3.6, 32p

Describes 10 disgusting foods people eat and what makes them gross.

Dogs and cats — Jenkins, Steve. {IL K-3, 636.7} — Houghton Mifflin, 2007, RL 5.2, 20p

Two related works, one about dogs with some comparisons to cats and one about cats with some comparisons to dogs.

Formula One cars — Schuette, Sarah L., 1976 — {IL 5-8, 629.228} — Capstone Press, 2007, RL 3, 32p

Brief text describes Formula One cars, including their main features, races, and drivers.

Gut-eating bugs: maggots reveal the time of death! — Denega, Danielle. {IL 5-8, 614} — Franklin Watts, 2007, RL 5.5, 64p

Profiles real-life cases that have been solved through forensic entomological evidence, and explores the career of a forensic entomologist.

Lungs: your respiratory system — Simon, Seymour. {IL 3-6, 612.2} — Smithsonian/Collins, 2007, RL 6.7, 30p

Provides information about the structure and function of the lungs and entire respiratory system, and discusses the importance of the lungs in providing the oxygen needed to sustain life.

A man for all seasons: the life of George Washington Carver — Krensky, Stephen. {IL K-3, 630} — Amistad, 2008, RL 4.8, 32p

Profiles the African American scientist George Washington Carver, who not only put the peanut on the map, but was also one of the first advocates of recycling.

The way we work: getting to know the amazing human body — Macaulay, David. {IL 5-8, 612} — Houghton Mifflin, 2008, RL 8.2, 336p

> A visual exploration of the inner workings of the human body that uses close-ups, cross-sections, and perspectives to look at the different body systems and how they function.

What the world eats — Menzel, Peter. {IL 5-8, 641.3} — Tricycle Press, 2008, RL 6.5, 160p

> A collection of photographs depicting twenty-five families from twenty-one different countries; includes Chad, Ecuador, Greenland, Japan, Mongolia, and others; and also describes the cost of a weeks worth of food, and other cultural information for each listed country.

Fine Arts (Art, Music, Sports) 700s

Title — Author. {Interest Level, Dewey Decimal Classification} — Publisher, Year, Reading Level, Number of Pages

---

At Gleason's gym — Lewin, Ted. {IL K-3, 796.83} — Roaring Brook Press, 2007, RL 2.9, 40p

> Looks at the action at Gleason's Gym in Brooklyn through the eyes of Sugar Boy, a nine-year-old boxing champion who is following in the footsteps of former Gleason's trainees like Muhammad Ali and Jake La Motta.

Campy: the story of Roy Campanella — Adler, David A. {IL K-3, 796.357} — Viking, 2007, RL 4.9, 32p

> Provides an illustrated biography of Roy Campanella, discussing his childhood, experience in the Negro Leagues, MLB career, the car accident that left him paralyzed, and his radio program.

The Great Race: the amazing round-the-world auto race of 1908 — Blackwood, Gary L. {IL 5-8, 796.72} — Abrams Books for Young Readers, 2008, RL 8.8, 141p

> Provides an account of the news-making contest to be the first to travel from New York to Paris by automobile, a race launched from four countries in 1908; and includes photographs, illustrations, and profiles of competitors.

Muhammad Ali: champion of the world — Winter, Jonah. {IL K-3, 796.83} — Schwartz & Wade Books, 2007, RL 3.9, 36p

Explores the life of legendary boxer Muhammad Ali, discussing how he trained to become a champion, converted to Islam, changed his name, refused to go to war, and won back his title.

Piano starts here: the young Art Tatum — Parker, Robert Andrew. {IL K-3, 786.2} — Schwartz & Wade Books, 2008, RL 2.2, 34p

Explores early twentieth-century jazz pianist and virtuoso Art Tatum's passion and talent for playing the instrument, and includes illustrations and biographical information.

Robot dreams — Varon, Sara. {IL 3-6, 741.5} — First Second, 2007, wordless, 205p

The enduring friendship between a dog and a robot is portrayed in this wordless graphic novel.

Sandy's circus: a story about Alexander Calder — Stone, Tanya Lee. {IL K-3, 730} — Viking, 2008, RL 3.6, 32p

An illustrated account of American mobile artist Alexander Calder's creation of a miniature circus from wire, string, rubber, cloth, and other found objects, which grew to fill multiple suitcases.

> Pair *Sandy's Circus* with *The Calder Game* by Blue Balliet. Engage your students by allowing them to create their own wire figures or mobiles.

Satchel Paige: striking out Jim Crow — Sturm, James. {IL 5-8, 741.5} — Hyperion/Jump at the Sun, 2007, RL 5.6, 89p

A graphic novel account of the career of Negro League pitcher Satchel Paige, discussing the show he put on as a popular player, as well as the respect he demanded as an African-American.

Sipping spiders through a straw: campfire songs for monsters — DiPucchio, Kelly S. {IL 3-6, 782.42164} — Scholastic Press, 2008, RL 3.2, 32p

A collection of creepy critters sing their favorite campfire sing-alongs, slightly altered for little monsters.

Spot 7 spooky — {IL K-3, 793.73} — Chronicle Books, 2007, RL 3.2, 32p

A collection of twelve pairs of seemingly identical spooky photographs, each containing seven differences the reader must find; includes riddles and challenges to find specific items.

Spot 7 toys — {IL 3-6, 790} — Chronicle Books, 2008, RL 2.4, 32p

Presents pairs of seemingly identical toy-themed photos, each containing differences the reader must find, and also includes riddles and challenges to find specific items on the right-hand pages.

Literature (Jokes, Riddles, and other Literary Works) 800s

Title — Author. {Interest Level, Dewey Decimal Classification} — Publisher, Year, Reading Level, Number of Pages

---

Awful Ogre running wild — Prelutsky, Jack. {IL K-3, 811} — Greenwillow Books, 2008, RL 3.5, 40p

A collection of poems recounting the awesome adventures Awful Ogre has during his summer vacation.

Birmingham, 1963 — Weatherford, Carole Boston. {IL 3-6, 811} — Wordsong, 2007, RL 4.6, 39p

Describes the feelings of a fictional character who witnessed the Sixteenth Street Baptist Church bombings in Birmingham, Alabama in 1963.

> Have students research the facts that are located within Weatherford's poems. Students will quickly see that even poetry may require research.

Good masters! Sweet ladies!: voices from a medieval village — Schlitz, Laura Amy. {IL 5-8, 812} — Candlewick Press, 2007, RL 5.9, 85p

A collection of short one-person plays featuring characters, between ten and fifteen years old, who live in or near a thirteenth-century English manor.

The laugh stand: adventures in humor — Cleary, Brian P. {IL 3-6, 817} — Millbrook Press, 2008, RL 3.7, 48p

An illustrated collection of Tom Swifties, daffynitions, pangrams, anagrams, and other wordplay jokes and cartoons.

My dog may be a genius: poems — Prelutsky, Jack. {IL K-3, 811} — Greenwillow Books, 2008, RL 3.2, 159p

A collection of poems by children's poet laureate Jack Prelutsky that celebrate the joys of childhood and the wackier side of life.

This is just to say: poems of apology and forgiveness — Sidman, Joyce. {IL 3-6, 811} — Houghton Mifflin, 2007, RL 3.9, 47p

A collection of poems written by a number of sixth-grade students who write poems of apology to someone, and a collection of responses in poetry form.

> Students may write their own apology letters and exchange them with someone else who will write the acceptance poem letter.

Tough boy sonatas — Crisler, Curtis L. {IL YA, 811} — Wordsong, 2007, RL 6.5, 86p

A collection of nearly forty poems that explores the struggles and joys of poor African-American boys in Gary, Indiana, reflecting the difficult circumstances they face.

> Crisler's book is an example of poetry that can be tough and realistic, showing students that not all poetry is Romeo and Juliet.

The trouble begins at 8: a life of Mark Twain in the wild, wild West — Fleischman, Sid. {IL 5-8, 818} — Greenwillow Books, 2008, RL 7.5, 224p

A narrative account of the childhood and youth of nineteenth-century writer Mark Twain.

Geography and History 900s
(See also chapter on War and History)

Title — Author. {Interest Level, Dewey Decimal Classification} — Publisher, Year, Reading Level, Number of Pages

---

> Help kids learn geography by having them mark places they read about on a wall map.

Ain't nothing but a man: my quest to find the real John Henry — Nelson, Scott Reynolds. {IL 5-8, 973} — National Geographic, 2008, RL 6.4, 64p

Historian Scott Nelson introduces children to the life of the real John Henry, drawing on songs, poems, and stories to describe the man behind the legendary African-American hero.

> Find versions of the folksong "John Henry." Group students and have them look for clues that may point to evidence of the real John Henry.

The book of time outs: a mostly true history of the world's biggest troublemakers — Lucke, Deb. {IL 3-6, 920.02} — Simon & Schuster Books for Young Readers, 2008, RL 6.0, 32p

A humorous collection of fourteen famous people in history who might have been considered trouble-makers and worthy of a "time-out."

A boy named Beckoning: the true story of Dr. Carlos Montezuma, Native American hero — Capaldi, Gina. {IL 3-6, 970.004} — Carolrhoda Books, 2008, RL 5.6, 32p

An illustrated exploration of the life of Carlos Montezuma which chronicles his childhood, in which he was kidnapped, sold into slavery, and adopted by an Italian photographer; relates what he learned when he set out to uncover his family's past; discusses his work as a doctor; and includes photographs.

Denied, detained, deported: stories from the dark side of immigration —
Bausum, Ann. {IL 5-8, 900} — National Geographic, 2008, RL 8.6, 111p

Discusses cases from the history of immigration in the U.S. in which immigrants are denied, such as the people aboard "The St. Louis" who were sent back to Nazi Germany during the Holocaust; the detained, such as Japanese Americans during WWII; and the deported, such as Emma Goldman, who was sent back to Russia in 1919 after living in the U.S. for thirty years.

Duel!: Burr and Hamilton's deadly war of words — Fradin, Dennis B. {IL 3-6, 973.4} — Walker & Co., 2008, RL 5.7, 36p

Examines the Burr-Hamilton duel which occurred on July 11, 1804, in which vice-president Aaron Burr and the secretary of treasury, Alexander Hamilton, used dueling pistols to settle their political grievances.

Farmer George plants a nation — Thomas, Peggy. {IL 3-6, 973.4} — Calkins Creek, 2008, RL 6.3, 40p

Describes how George Washington built his farm at Mount Vernon, discussing his experiments with seeds, fertilizers, and tools and presenting related letters and diary entries.

Go, go America — Yaccarino, Dan. {IL 3-6, 973} — Scholastic Press, 2008, RL 5.9, 71p

Presents hundreds of unique facts about each of the states, describing strange festivals, traditions, contests, laws, people, and landmarks across the country.

King George: what was his problem?: everything your schoolbooks didn't tell you about the American Revolution — Sheinkin, Steve. {IL 5-8, 973.3} — Roaring Brook Press, 2008, 2005, RL 6.5, 195p

Presents an informal history of the American Revolution, covering the Stamp Act, Paul Revere, and the battle of Ticonderoga, and includes extracts from letters, memorable quotes, and line illustrations.

More bones — Olson, Arielle North. {IL 3-6, 398} — Viking Children's Books, 2008, RL 5.3, 176p

A collection of scary stories collected from civilizations around the globe and throughout history.

Pharaoh: life and afterlife of a God — Kennett, David. {IL 5-8, 932} — Walker & Co., 2008, RL 7.1, 48p

> Provides an account of the lives of Egyptian pharaohs Seti I and his son, Ramesses II, looking at the civilizations they created, and discussing the elaborate preparations they made for their deaths and burials in anticipation of being transformed into complete gods in the afterlife.

The real Benedict Arnold — Murphy, Jim. {IL 5-8, 973.3} — Clarion Books, 2007, RL 8.9, 264p

> Presents a comprehensive biography and history of Benedict Arnold that examines many of his heroic deeds and contributions to the Revolutionary cause before he decided to switch sides.

Real pirates: the untold story of the Whydah from slave ship to pirate ship — Clifford, Barry. {IL 5-8, 910.4} — National Geographic, 2008, RL 8.4, 32p

> An illustrated exploration of the eighteenth-century ship "Whydah," which discusses its use as a slave ship, its capture by pirates, and its sinking in Cape Cod in 1717 and describes artifacts from its wreck site.

Texas Rangers: legendary lawmen — Spradlin, Michael P. {IL K-3, 976.4} — Walker & Co., 2008, RL 5.5, 32p

> Describes the history of the Texas Rangers, a law enforcement agency based out of Austin, Texas, and profiles famous rangers.

The tomb of King Tutankhamen — Woods, Michael. {IL 5-8, 932} — Twenty-First Century Books, 2008, RL 6.7, 80p

> Offers a brief introduction to the 1922 discovery of King Tut's tomb in Egypt's Valley of the Kings, describing how archaeologist Howard Carter discovered the tomb and spent the next ten years excavating the priceless artifacts that had been buried with the pharaoh.

The wall: growing up behind the Iron Curtain — Sis, Peter. {IL 3-6, 943.7} — Frances Foster Books, 2007, RL 3.2, 50p

> Artist Sis Peter describes what it was like growing up in a Communist country and discusses how Western culture influenced his life.

Web Connections

Publisher Sites

Capstone Press <http://www.capstonepress.com>

Don't Know Much About series <http://www.dontknowmuch.com/kids/index.html>

Fact Hound: A Web Portal of Kid Friendly sites, sponsored by Capstone Publishers, provides an internet search tool of grade appropriate websites at no charge <http://www.facthound.com/>

Heinemann Raintree Publishers for a newsletter about weeding nonfiction, as well as nonfiction series books for K-12 <http://www.heinemannlibrary.com/>

Magazines

Book Links Magazine <http://ala.org/ala/productsandpublications/periodicals/booklinks/booklinks.htm>

National Geographic (see also NG for Kids) <http://www.nationalgeographic.com/>

Authors

Deborah Hopkinson <http://www.deborahhopkinson.com/>

Seymour Simon <http://www.seymoursimon.com/>

For Kids

KidsClick: Kid Friendly websites divided into Dewey Classes <http://sunsite.berkeley.edu/KidsClick!/>

KidSpace @ the Internet Public Library (Science Fair Project Guide) <http://ipl.si.umich.edu/youth/projectguide>

National Gallery of Art Kid's <http://www.nga.gov/kids>

For Teachers and Librarians

Children's Book Press for multicultural lesson plans <http://childrensbookpress.org/teachersguide>

National Council of Social Studies for lists of annual notable books for K-12 and national standards < http://www.socialstudies.org/>

National Council of Teachers of Math for lessons and national standards <http://www.nctm.org/>

National Science Teachers Association for lists of annual notable books for K-12 and links to national standards <http://www.nsta.org/>

CHAPTER 2

A Picture Paints a Thousand Words: Graphic Works

Graphic novels are one of the most popular genres for *all* kids, not just boys. What, exactly, are they? Graphic novels are books that are written and illustrated in the style of a comic book. They have short dialogue and framed boxes of illustration. Today's readers, especially reluctant ones, can use graphic novels to grow as a reader. Readers must rely on the pictures and follow the sequence in order for the story to make sense. Many of these books are series, building in a repeat audience.

However, some graphic works may not be appropriate for all readers. Just like other genres, there are YA and Adult graphic novels. Teachers and parents need to be aware of what is available in order to steer kids in the best direction. Be prepared to make mistakes—we all do. If you do, you can always return the book to the company or send it to a higher institution of learning. Be willing to take a chance on a genre that can really hook your readers.

Graphic works can also be used in the classroom to teach the same curriculum standards as traditional literature because point of view, setting, character, and plot are integral to graphic novels as well. Publishers are using the interest of the format in nonfiction as well. Capstone Press has a line of books that are part graphic novel, part fiction. These versions make it easier for English Language Learners (ELL) to grasp the storyline, as well as give them some background for reading the original. Stone Arch books and Capstone Press have created Graphic Libraries of content related curriculum. Many of their series are available in Spanish. Now students can read what they want, but learn something while doing it.

Teacher/Librarian Strategies:

- Use a document camera to "read" a graphic work to your students. The pictures are as important as the text, so everyone needs to see both well.

- Have students visit Mo Willem's website and learn to draw the pigeon. Then they can write their own pigeon stories

- Visit Dav Pilkey's site to learn how to draw cartoon characters.

- Preview all new series before displaying to students.

- Learn to recognize controversial publishers and authors if you are concerned about age appropriateness. The University Library of Buffalo has a website that explains the focus of publishers which may help you learn which companies are grade appropriate for your students. For elementary educators, you may want to read *Comics for Kids* by Michele Gorman, published by Linworth.

- If you are a media specialist, perhaps you could add a statement to your collection development policy about the inclusion of graphic works to your collection.

- In the library, instead of barcoding comic books, have students sign for them on a clipboard—perhaps as a reward or over the weekend. You could also use a generic barcoded envelope to check out small materials like these, allowing you to keep records but speeding up the processing steps.

- Allow students who like to draw the opportunity to use their skills in their work.

- Graphic novels and comic books are expensive. Encourage your students to swap books with each other.

- Have a cartoon day. Read the funny papers. Read comic books. Share one of the graphic picture books listed below.

- Have students illustrate—graphic novel style—an event they are studying in social studies.

- Allow students to copy and draw characters from their books. That's how they learn. Artists like Mo Willems visit schools and teach them that their drawings are different from others. The more they practice, the better the get.

- Use the computer to create stories with digital graphics. Comic Life by Plasq software is an inexpensive subscription service. You can get it for either Mac or Windows.

- Have an Anime Afternoon: watch anime, snack, raffle card packs, do word searches.

- Create SuperHero bodies as part of your writing assignments. Use a digital headshot photo for each student and have them create their Super Bodies. Students must write about their super trait.

- As a tie-in to Captain Underpants, conduct an Underwear Olympics. Wearing size 9x underwear, students participate in various relays and games.

- Let kids go to the new website from the makers of Where's Waldo. <http://www.thegreatpicturehunt.com/>

Books with Cartoons and Graphics

Title — Author. {Interest Level, Dewey Decimal Classification} — Publisher, Year, Reading Level, Number of Pages

---

20,000 leagues under the sea — Bowen, Carl. {IL 5-8, 741.5} — Stone Arch Books, 2008, RL 3, 63p

A graphic novel adaptation of Jules Verne's classic story that finds scientist Pierre Aronnax and his servant held captive by Nemo, the captain of the high-tech submarine, "Nautilus."

Take advantage of kids' interest in Jules Verne (thanks to the *Journey to the Center* movie). See Walden Media for a complete [free] teacher's guide to the movie.

The adventures of Daniel Boom, a.k.a. Loud Boy. 1, Sound off! — Steinberg, David. {IL 3-6, 741.5} — Grosset & Dunlap, 2008, RL 5.6, upaged

> Daniel Boom, a kid with no volume control, becomes Loud Boy and fights the Kid-Rid Corporation, which has silenced the world with a machine called the Soundsucker LX.

The arrival — Tan, Shaun. {IL 5-8, -Fic-} — A. A. Levine, 2007, wordless, unpaged

> In this wordless graphic novel, a man leaves his homeland and sets off for a new country, where he must build a new life for himself and his family.

Artemis Fowl: the graphic novel — Colfer, Eoin. {IL 5-8, 741.5} — Hyperion Books for Children, 2007, RL 5.9, unpaged

> A graphic novel adaptation of Eoin Colfer's novel in which a twelve-year-old evil genius tries to restore his family fortune by capturing a fairy and demanding a ransom in gold, but the fairies fight back with magic, technology, and a particularly nasty troll.

Beowulf — Hinds, Gareth. {IL 5-8, 741.5} — Candlewick Press, 2007, RL 6.5, unpaged

> Presents a graphic novel adaptation of the Old English epic poem, "Beowulf," in which a Norse hero saves Denmark's royal house from monsters, returns home to become his own people's greatest king, and then faces a murderous dragon to protect them.

Bone 7, Ghost circles — Smith, Jeff. {IL 3-6, 741.5} — Graphix, 2008, RL 6.8, 150p

> The Bone cousins, along with Gran'ma Ben and Thorn, struggle to reach the safety of the city of Atheia, on a journey that has become increasingly bleak with the release of the Lord of the Locusts.

Play a Bone-based video game at Scholastic. Gamers playing "Whac-a-rat," must aim a sling shot at the bad guys to earn points.

Boys of steel: the creators of Superman — Nobleman, Marc Tyler. {IL 5-8, 741.5} — Knopf, 2008, RL 5, 34p

> Relates the story of Cleveland teenagers Jerry Siegel and Joe Shuster's creation of Superman.

The castaways — Vollmar, Rob. {IL YA, 741.5} — NBM/ComicsLit, 2007, unpaged

> Thirteen-year-old Tucker Freeman, driven from his home in 1932 by his mean, spinster aunt, hops a passing train where he is befriended by Elijah, an elderly African-American man who cares for the boy and convinces him to return home to his mother.

Chaucer's Canterbury tales — Williams, Marcia. {IL 3-6, 821} — Candlewick Press, 2007, RL 5.3, 45p

> A retelling of Geoffrey Chaucer's famous work in which a group of pilgrims in fourteenth-century England tell each other stories as they travel on a pilgrimage to the cathedral at Canterbury.

Comic book century: the history of American comic books — Krensky, Stephen. {IL 5-8, 741.5} — Twenty-First Century Books, 2008, RL 8.9, 112p

> Provides a history of comic books in America during the twentieth century, showing how they have influenced and been influenced by American culture, and includes an epilogue about comics in the early twenty-first century.

Diary of a wimpy kid: Greg Heffley's journal — Kinney, Jeff. {IL 5-8, -Fic-} — Amulet Books, 2007, RL 5, 217p

> Greg records his sixth grade experiences in a middle school where he and his best friend, Rowley, undersized weaklings amid boys who need to shave twice daily, hope just to survive, but when Rowley grows more popular, Greg must take drastic measures to save their friendship.

> Did you know that you can read *Diary of a Wimpy Kid* online for free at FunBrain.com?

Don't let the pigeon stay up late! — Willems, Mo. {IL K-3, -E-} — Hyperion Books for Children, 2006, RL 2.1, 36p

A pigeon fights yawns while coming up with many reasons why it should be allowed to stay up late.

> Learn how to draw the pigeon at Hyperion's website. There is also a link to an 8 page teacher's guide to *Pigeon Finds a Hotdog*. See end of chapter.

Dracula — Mucci, Michael. {IL YA, 741.5} — Sterling, 2008, RL 5.0, unpaged

A graphic novel adaptation of Bram Stoker's *Dracula* in which Jonathan Harker travels to Transylvania, where he meets the eccentric Count Dracula and uncovers an ancient evil.

The explosive world of volcanoes with Max Axiom, super scientist — Harbo, Christopher L. {IL 5-8, 551.21} — Capstone Press, 2008, RL 5.1, 32p

Max Axiom teaches the science of volcanoes, traveling the world to explore how they form, what makes them erupt, and other topics.

Houdini: the handcuff king — Lutes, Jason. {IL 5-8, 793.8} — Hyperion Paperbacks, 2008, RL 4.6, 81p

A brief biography of escape artist Harry Houdini written in graphic comic format that reveals the secrets of some of his stunts.

The invention of Hugo Cabret: a novel in words and pictures — Selznick, Brian. {IL 3-6, -Fic-} — Scholastic Press, 2007, RL 6, 533p

When twelve-year-old Hugo, an orphan living and repairing clocks within the walls of a Paris train station in 1931, meets a mysterious toyseller and his goddaughter, his undercover life and his biggest secret are jeopardized.

> Go to the book's website and follow the links to the Caldecott acceptance speech. There you will see a video of Hugo getting the phone call and taking a plane to Anaheim to receive his award. Selznick has incredible information on his website about early movies and automatons.

The legend of Sleepy Hollow — Zornow, Jeff. {IL 3-6, 741.5} — Magic Wagon, 2008, RL 4.9, 32p

A graphic novel adaptation of "The Legend of Sleepy Hollow," the story of Ichabod Crane, an irritating schoolteacher who falls prey to his own superstitious belief in a terrifying headless horseman.

Like a Pro: 101 simple ways to do really important stuff — Becker, Helanie {IL 3-6, 646.7} — Maple Tree Press, 2006, RL 5.0, 160p

Presents a collection of illustrated step-by-step instructions performing a wide range of tasks, from changing a bike tire and baking chocolate cookies, to drawing cartoons and taking professional photographs.

Stage a debate. Are graphic novels literature? Should we have them in libraries? Why or why not?

Mary Shelley's Frankenstein — Burgan, Michael. {IL 5-8, 741.5} — Stone Arch Books, 2008, RL 3, 63p

A retelling of Mary Shelley's classic horror story "Frankenstein" written in graphic novel format.

The mighty 12: superheroes of Greek myth — Smith, Charles R. {IL 3-6, 292.2} — Little, Brown, 2008, RL 6.4, 48p

Introduces an illustrated collection of twelve mythical gods and goddesses of ancient Greece including Zeus, Apollo, Aphrodite, Athena, and Dionysus.

The pigeon wants a puppy! — Willems, Mo. {IL K-3, -E-} — Hyperion Books for Children, 2008, RL 1.2, 34p

The pigeon really, really wants a puppy, but when a puppy arrives the pigeon changes its mind.

The *Pigeon* books are all about persuasion. Ask older students to analyze the different types of persuasion that the pigeon uses. Students must support their answers with specific quotes from the book.

Robot dreams — Varon, Sara. {IL 3-6, 741.5} — First Second, 2007, wordless, 205p

The enduring friendship between a dog and a robot is portrayed in this wordless graphic novel.

Sardine in outer space. 3 — Guibert, Emmanuel. {IL 3-6, 741.5} — First Second, 2007, RL 3.4, 102p

Sardine and Little Louie go head-to-head with a shrunken, but still powerful, Supermuscleman in the Space Boxing Championship.

Satchel Paige: striking out Jim Crow — Sturm, James. {IL 5-8, 741.5} — Hyperion/Jump at the Sun, 2007, RL 5.6, 89p

A graphic novel account of the career of Negro League pitcher Satchel Paige, discussing the show he put on as a popular player, as well as the respect he demanded as an African-American.

Spider-Man: the menace of Mysterio — Raicht, Mike. {IL 3-6, 741.5} — Marvel, 2006, RL 2.7, unpaged

Spider-Man, framed for a rash of robberies, learns he has been set up by a con man who is passing himself off as the superhero Mysterio. *(Spider-Man series)*

SuperHero ABC — McLeod, Bob. {IL K-3, -E-} — HarperCollins, 2006, RL 2.7, 34p

Humorously-named superheroes such as Goo Girl and The Volcano represent the letters of the alphabet from A to Z.

> Create SuperHeroes of your own. What are their powers? Who is their enemy? What are their weaknesses?

Thoreau at Walden — Thoreau, Henry David. {IL 5-8, 741.5} — Hyperion, 2008, RL 6.6, 99p

A graphic novel interpretation of Henry David Thoreau's "Walden," featuring the actual words from the text in which Thoreau describes his experiment in simple living.

Town boy — Lat. {IL YA, 741.5} — First Second, 2007, RL 2.6, 191p

An illustrated continuation of the story of Mat, a Malaysian teenager who moves from his small village to attend boarding school in the nearby city of Ipoh, where he is introduced to modern music, busy streets, first love, and a growing passion for art.

Traction man meets Turbodog — Grey, Mini. {IL K-3, -E-} — Alfred A. Knopf, 2008, RL 3.4, unpaged

Traction Man braves the evil bin things in order to save Scrubbing Brush, who had been thrown away by the little boy's father and replaced with a battery-operated dog.

You can draw Marvel characters — Jurgens, Dan. {IL 5-8, 741.5} — DK, 2006, RL 5.0, 96p

A step-by-step guide to drawing Marvel-style comic characters that covers the male and female figure, body perspective, heads, hands, feet, and clothing as well as monsters, battle scenes, light, shading, shots and angles, and layout; provides case examples of Spider-Man, Storm, and Wolverine; includes sections on inking and coloring; and features trace overlays. *(You Can Draw series)*

You can never find a Rickshaw when it Monsoons: the world on one cartoon a day — Willems, Mo. {IL YA, 741.5} — Hyperion Paperbacks, 2006, 393p

A collection of single panel comics that the author/illustrator used to record his daily impressions of places he visited while on a year-long journey around the world following his college graduation.

Web Connections

ALA/Comic Books and Graphic Novels: Internet Links <http://www.ala.org/ala/acrl/acrlpubs/crlnews/backissues2005/february05/comicbooks.htm>

Brodart: Kid-Safe Graphic Novels for Your Readers <http://www.graphicnovels.brodart.com/>

Comic Books for Young Adults: A Guide for Librarians <http://ublib.buffalo.edu/lml/comics/pages/>

Fun Brain (Diary of a Wimpy Kid Online Journal) <http://www.funbrain.com/journal/Journal.html?ThisJournalDay=1&ThisPage=1>

Hyperion: Draw the Pigeon <http://www.hyperionbooksforchildren.com/board/displaybook.asp?id=1351>

Mo Willems: The Pigeon Man <http://www.mowillems.com/>

Scholastic (Whac-a-Rat) <http://www.scholastic.com/bone/whac.htm>

Stone Arch Books: Safe Graphic Novels <http://www.stonearchbooks.com/>

Using Graphic Novels in the Classroom: A Free PDF Booklet <http:// www.boneville.dreamhosters.com/wp/wp-content/uploads/2006/05/Bone_Teachers_Guide.pdf>

YALSA: Great Graphic Novels for Teens <http://www.ala.org/ala/yalsa/booklistsawards/greatgraphicnovelsforteens/gn.htm>

CHAPTER 3

And He Scores: Sports

No doubt about it. Sports are important to many boys. True, many girls enjoy sports as well. Hand out the local newspaper to a classroom of students and generally, boys will go straight to the sports section. When older boys are asked, "If you aren't reading, what are you doing with your time?" they will quite often reply that they are on a sports team. Just recently I attended a middle school book club and half of the boys who are usually there were absent because they were playing baseball. When the World Cup is on TV, the streets of Rome are empty, but the air is filled with sounds of people watching the event at home or in businesses. It stands to reason that we should supply interested students with material on one of their favorite subjects.

One way we can do that is to provide magazines and newspapers in our classrooms and libraries. I spoke about books and boys in Alaska at a public library. The event was covered by the local newspaper. When I asked the photographer (who was a young man) if he was a reader, his response was, "Oh, no, just the newspaper." My response was, "Since when is reading the newspaper not reading?" Many people have a misconception about what a reader is. Don't we have to read to absorb the contents of the newspaper? Don't we have to read when we surf the Web? If we are going to be successful in our endeavors, we must dispel the notion that real readers only read novels.

So purchase *Sports Illustrated* for your library or classroom. For elementary schools you can purchase *SI for Kids*. Encourage students to visit SI websites to check on scores, take the polls, or read the articles. Teachers and media specialists may want to visit sports websites themselves from time to time and post material in the classroom or school library where students who don't have computer access at home can see it.

Classroom teachers can participate in Newspaper in Education programs <http://www.nieonline.com/>. Contact your local newspaper to receive free or inexpensive sets of papers to use in your classes. Plan your curriculum related lessons using the papers as your text. You will be teaching the same standards, but using a medium that is more likely to reach a reluctant reader. Lesson plans are available on the NIE site.

A teacher of middle school students who read at second grade level asked me how he could teach his boys to read. In our conversation, the newspaper came up. It seemed that his students brought the newspaper into class and skimmed it every day. I recommended that he ask students to use box scores to write sentences. He could cut the caption off the pictures and have students match the picture to the caption. The ideas are endless, the material current, and the enthusiasm will grow. Learning to read will grow out of a desire to read the material.

Sports books are easy enough to find in the school library; they are in the 790s. When evaluating the books you have, be sure to check the copyright dates for safety rules that may have changed since the printing of the book. Students will rarely want to read sports books with black and white pictures, so you may want to weed those as well. Check with your publisher representatives for updates on new sports series nonfiction books.

Students who like to read about sports may want to be introduced to writers of sports fiction. Authors like Dan Gutman, Mike Lupica, and Tim Green write sports fiction series. Teach students to use the online library catalog to find them by teaching keyword searches like "baseball fiction." Teachers and librarians should again look at their collection and evaluate the "desire factor." Will students want to read it just because it is sports? Outdated illustrations, yellowed pages and musty smells will turn away the most ardent sports fan. Matt Christopher is one of our classic sports fiction writers, but it may be time to update those oldies for the newer versions.

Teacher/Librarian Strategies:

- Bring sports into the library or classroom by using the idea of a game or contest to interest your students.

- Provide non-traditional activities for students: chess, checkers, board games, or puzzles. Cracker Barrel has a fabulous checker game rug. Middle schools in San Diego Unified School District have tournaments scheduled because it is so popular with their boys.

- Turn any information seeking exercise into a race. "One-two-three go!" creates enthusiasm even for mundane tasks.

- Evaluate content learned at the end of a unit by having students prepare questions and answers for a Jeopardy or Millionaire game. A classroom teacher has created a PowerPoint template that you can use for creating your own game. See end of chapter for the URL.

- Provide other reading material that features sports. Purchase *Sports Illustrated*, *SI for Kids*, skateboarding magazines, and newspapers.

- Provide your PE teacher with a bibliography of support books or read-alouds. Better yet, give her a packet that includes the books and lesson plans.

- Ask your PE teachers or coaches to read to your classes.

- Invite local sports reporters or athletes to read to your classes or talk about how they write in their work.

- Celebrate sports events by connecting them to your reading or language arts curriculum. Students can write letters or send email to their favorite players. They can make posters advertising their team.

- If you use a computer reading program, like Accelerated Reader, be sure that you have plenty of sports-related books that are interesting for your students. Nothing turns off a reader like a terrible book with a test on it.

- Host a Reading Marathon. Southside High School in Elmira, New York broke a Guinness World Record in 2006 by reading aloud for 128 hours straight. Students read in one hour shifts, reading aloud favorites such as the *Harry Potter* series and ending with *Oh! The Places You'll Go* by Dr. Seuss.

- Host a BMX bike stunt show. Try contacting your local bike dealer about professionals in the area who would do a demonstration of stunts and safety for your students.

- Have a martial arts demonstration in the library and display the appropriate books.

- Have a skateboard night, inviting representatives from local stores or parks to discuss skateboard assembly and safety.

- Many times your local minor or major league teams will offer free clinics for interested students. Be sure to advertise.

- Have a weight lifting clinic sponsored by your local high school. Contact the USA Weightlifting Organization who may be willing to host a presentation to athletes and coaches at area high schools on the technique of important and functional strength training exercises.

- Have a Yo-Yo contest.

- Host a bike clinic, offering repair and tune-ups.

And He Scores: Books about Sports

Title — Author. {Interest Level, Dewey Decimal Classification} — Publisher, Year, Reading Level, Number of Pages

Ballet of the elephants — Schubert, Leda. {IL K-3, 796.8} — Roaring Brook Press, 2006, RL 3.8, 32p

Tells the story of how circus owner John Ringling North, choreographer George Balanchine, and composer Igor Stravinsky teamed up to create the "Circus Polka," a ballet for fifty elephants and fifty dancers, and describes the opening night performance in 1942.

> Find a recording of the "Circus Polka" to share with your students.

Baseball crazy: ten short stories that cover all the bases — {IL 5-8, -Fic-} — Dial Books for Young Readers, 2008, RL 6.5, 191p

> A collection of ten short stories from popular, contemporary authors that celebrate the joys of America's favorite past-time and the wonder, frustration, and delight of its fans.

Beanball — Fehler, Gene. {IL YA, -Fic-} — Clarion Books, 2008, RL 4.4, 119p

> Relates, from diverse points of view, events surrounding the critical injury of popular and talented high school athlete, Luke "Wizard" Wallace, when he is hit in the face by a fastball.

The big field — Lupica, Mike. {IL 5-8, -Fic-} — Philomel Books, 2008, RL 4.4, 243p

> When fourteen-year-old baseball player Hutch feels threatened by the arrival of a new teammate named Darryl, he tries to work through his insecurities about both Darryl and his remote and silent father, who was once a great ballplayer too.

The big game of everything — Lynch, Chris. {IL YA, -Fic-} — HarperTeen, 2008, RL 5.0, 275p

> Jock looks forward to spending two months of the summer working at his grandfather's golf complex, but when the rest of his eccentric family go with him they all learn a lesson about the bond of family.

Casey at the bat — Thayer, Ernest Lawrence. {IL YA, 811} — KCP Poetry, 2006, RL 5.3, 32p

> Presents Ernest L. Thayer's famous poem "Casey at the Bat," revamped through illustrations to tell the story of a heated ball game played by inner-city teenagers at an urban park. *(From the Visions in Poetry series, graphically illustrated classic poems)*

Casey back at bat — Gutman, Dan. {IL K-3, -E-} — HarperCollins, 2007, RL 3.6, 32p

> Presents a humorous sequel to Ernest Lawrence Thayer's classic "Casey at the Bat" with colorful illustrations and rhyming text.

Students may not appreciate the humor of Gutman's story if they have not heard the original. Be sure to share it with them first. You could easily use *Back at Bat* in Social Studies, as there are references to Social Studies content in the plot.

Cork & Fuzz: good sports — Chaconas, Dori. {IL K-3, -E-} — Viking, 2007, RL 1.4, 26p

Short-legged Cork is upset when tall Fuzz wins every game they play, until he learns that their friendship is more important than winning.

Dirt bike racer — Christopher, Matt. {IL 3-6, -Fic-} — Norwood House Press, 2008, RL 4.5, 152p

Twelve-year-old Ron Baker finds a minibike while scuba diving and, with the help of a former motorcycle rider and racer, restores the bike and enters a competition.

Did you know? Matt Christopher died in 1997. His son, Dale, continues to write the best-selling sports series.

Dunk under pressure — Wallace, Rich. {IL 5-8, -Fic-} — Viking, 2006, RL 4.5, 119p

Free throw specialist Cornell "Dunk" Duncan joins the YMCA summer basketball league all-star team, but after losing his confidence in an important game the seventh-grader makes some decisions about becoming an all-around player. *(Book 7, Winning Season series)*

Extreme skydiving — Kalman, Bobbie. {IL 3-6, 797.5} — Crabtree Pub., 2006, RL 6.1, 32p

Describes extreme skydiving and moves, the sport's history, and some of its major forms and fliers. *(From Extreme Sports series)*

Face-off — Maddox, Jake. {IL 5-8, -Fic-} — Stone Arch Books, 2007, RL 3.2, 65p

Kyle wants to be a great hockey player just like his older brother, but to do that, he must focus all of his energy on the game and not be distracted by a teammate's injury.

Football genius — Green, Tim. {IL 5-8, -Fic-} — HarperTrophy, 2008, RL 4.8, 244p

Troy, a sixth-grader with an unusual gift for predicting football plays before they occur, attempts to use his ability to help his favorite team, the Atlanta Falcons, but he must first prove himself to the coach and players.

Formula One cars — Schuette, Sarah L. {IL 5-8, 629.228} — Capstone Press, 2007, RL 3, 32p

Brief text describes Formula One cars, including their main features, races, and drivers.

Free baseball — Corbett, Sue. {IL 3-6, -Fic-} — Dutton Children's Books, 2006, RL 6.4, 152p

Eleven-year-old Felix becomes a bat boy for a minor league baseball team, hoping to someday be like his father, a famous Cuban outfielder.

Game — Myers, Walter Dean. {IL YA, -Fic-} — HarperTeen, 2008, RL 4.9, 218p

Drew Lawson, counting on basketball to get him into college and out of Harlem, struggles to keep his cool when the coach brings in two white players and puts them in positions that clearly threaten Drew's game.

Go big or go home — Hobbs, Will. {IL 5-8, -Fic-} — HarperCollins, 2008, RL 5.6, 185p

Fourteen-year-old Brady and his cousin Quinn love extreme sports, but nothing could prepare them for the aftermath of Brady's close encounter with a meteorite after it crashes into his Black Hills, South Dakota bedroom.

Hard hit — Turner, Ann Warren. {IL YA, -Fic-} — Scholastic Press, 2006, RL 5.1, 167p

A rising high school baseball star faces his most difficult challenge when his father is diagnosed with pancreatic cancer.

Heat — Lupica, Mike. {IL 5-8, -Fic-} — Philomel Books, 2006, RL 6.9, 220p

Pitching prodigy Michael Arroyo is on the run from social services after being banned from playing Little League baseball because rival coaches doubt he is only twelve years old and he has no parents to offer them proof.

Watch the MSNBC video interview of the author with Matt Lauer regarding the idea of the story. Talk with kids about parental pressure to succeed in sports.

Jackie's bat — Lorbiecki, Marybeth. {IL K-3, -E-} — Simon & Schuster Books for Young Readers, 2006, RL 2.3, 35p

Joey, the batboy for the Brooklyn Dodgers in 1947, learns a hard lesson about respect for people of different races after Jackie Robinson joins the team.

Jim & me: a baseball card adventure — Gutman, Dan. {IL 5-8, -Fic-} — HarperCollins, 2008, RL 5.2, 195p

Joe and his longtime enemy, Bobby Fuller, use a vintage baseball card to travel in time, hoping to stop Jim Thorpe from participating in the 1912 Olympics and losing his medals, but instead they watch Thorpe struggle during his first season with the New York Giants.

Jim Thorpe: original All-American — Bruchac, Joseph. {IL 5-8, 796.092} — Dial Books/Walden Media, 2006, RL 5.8, 288p

Focusing on Jim Thorpe's years at Carlisle, this book brings his early athletic career—and especially his college football days—to life, while also dispelling some myths about him and movingly depicting the Native American experience at the turn of the twentieth century.

Kicker — Bossley, Michele Martin. {IL 5-8, -Fic-} — Orca Book Publishers, 2007, RL 3, 143p

Best friends and soccer teammates Izzy and Julia team up with their coach's son and Izzy's crush Drew to discover who is threatening Julia, and why someone is trying to sabotage their practice field.

Orca Book Publishers specializes in quality books for reluctant readers. They offer many series with high interest-low vocabulary for secondary level readers.

Kickoff! — Barber, Tiki. {IL 3-6, 796.332} — Simon & Schuster Books for Young Readers, 2007, RL 4.7, 156p

> Twelve-year-olds Tiki and Ronde tryout for the junior high football team and hope to not only get a spot but also to be a part of the starting lineup.

The Kingfisher soccer encyclopedia — Gifford, Clive. {IL 5-8, 796.33403} — Kingfisher, 2006, RL 5.0, 144p

> An encyclopedia of soccer with profiles of the world's greatest teams and soccer's legendary players, from Alfredo di Stefano to Mia Hamm.

Lay-ups and long shots: an anthology of short stories — {IL 5-8, -Fic-} — Darby Creek Pub., 2008, RL 6.2, 112p

> A collection of nine short stories about sports by various authors, including David Lubar, Joseph Bruchac, and Terry Trueman.

The million dollar goal — Gutman, Dan {IL 3-6, -Fic-} — Hyperion, 2006, RL 5.4, 176p

> 11-year-old fraternal twins Dusk and Dawn have an opportunity to win a million dollars by shooting a goal after a Montreal Canadiens hockey game. *(From the Million Dollar Book series)*

The million dollar putt — Gutman, Dan. {IL 3-6, -Fic-} — Hyperion Books for Children, 2006, RL 6.4, 169p

> Assisted by his neighbor, Birdie, blind thirteen-year-old Ed "Bogie" Bogard will win one million dollars if he can sink a ten-foot putt in Hawaii's fifth annual Angus Killick Memorial Tournament. *(From the Million Dollar Book series)*

> Dan has written over 65 books. Go to his website and read some of his rejection letters.

The million dollar shot — Gutman, Dan. {IL 3-6, -Fic-} — Hyperion, 2006, RL 4.8, 128p

> Eddie and his friend, Annie, learn of a poetry contest sponsored by Finkle Foods. The winner of the contest gets an opportunity to sink a foul shot during halftime at the NBA finals and win one million dollars. *(From the Million Dollar Book series)*

Out of the ballpark — Rodriguez, Alex. {IL K-3, -E-} — HarperCollins, 2007, RL 2.3, 32p

Although Alex is nervous about his role in the approaching baseball playoffs and championship game, he soon figures out how to fix his mistakes and become a better player.

Out standing in my field — Jennings, Patrick. {IL 5-8, -Fic-} — Scholastic, 2006, RL 6.8, 165p

Eleven year old, Ty Cutter loves baseball, but he is just not cut out to play the game.

The penalty — Peet, Mal. {IL YA, -Fic-} — Candlewick Press, 2007, RL 5.4, 262p

Sports reporter Paul Faustino reluctantly investigates the disappearance of a young soccer star from San Juan who hasn't been seen since he missed a winning penalty kick during a big game, and unknowingly the journalist becomes entangled in a world of slavery and the occult.

Rally cars — Braulick, Carrie A. {IL 5-8, 796.7} — Capstone Press, 2007, RL 3.1, 32p

Photographs and simple text describe rally cars, their main features, and how they are built.

Rash — Hautman, Pete. {IL YA, -Fic-} — Simon & Schuster Books for Young Readers, 2006, RL 4.7, 249p

In a future society that has decided it would "rather be safe than free," sixteen-year-old Bo's anger management problems land him in a tundra jail where he survives with the help of his running skills and an artificial intelligence program named Bork.

Samurai Shortstop — Gratz, Alan. {IL YA, -Fic-} — Penguin Group, 2006, RL 4.9, 288p

While obtaining a Western education at a prestigious Japanese boarding school in 1890, sixteen-year-old Toyo also receives traditional samurai training which has profound effects on both his baseball game and his relationship with his father.

Satchel Paige: don't look back — Adler, David A. {IL K-3, 796.357} — Harcourt, 2007, RL 4.5, 32p

Colorful illustrations and simple text tell the story of the life and baseball career of legendary pitcher Satchel Paige from his time with the Negro Leagues to his years with the American League.

Satchel Paige: striking out Jim Crow — Sturm, James. {IL 5-8, 741.5} — Hyperion/Jump at the Sun, 2007, RL 5.6, 89p

A graphic novel account of the career of Negro League pitcher Satchel Paige, discussing the show he put on as a popular player, as well as the respect he demanded as an African-American.

Saturday night dirt — Weaver, Will. {IL YA, -Fic-} — Farrar, Straus and Giroux, 2008, RL 4.7, 163p

In a small town in northern Minnesota, the much-anticipated Saturday night dirt-track race at the old-fashioned, barely viable, Headwaters Speedway becomes, in many ways, an important life-changing event for all the participants on and off the track.

Saving the world and other extreme sports — Patterson, James. {IL YA, -Fic-} — Little, Brown, 2007, RL 4.8, 405p

The time has come for Max, Fang, Iggy, Nudge, Gasman, and Angel to face their ultimate enemy and, despite many obstacles, try to save the world from a sinister plan to re-engineer a select population into a scientifically superior master race.

Scrubs forever! — McEwan, James. {IL 3-6, -Fic-} — Darby Creek Pub., 2008, RL 3.4, 63p

Dan is about to give up wrestling when he discovers that he really likes rock climbing; however, he starts to take it too seriously when winning becomes too important.

Shakespeare bats cleanup — Koertge, Ronald. {IL YA, -Fic-} — Candlewick Press, 2006, RL 3.8, 128p

When a fourteen-year-old baseball player catches mono, he sets aside his glove and picks up a pen to write poetry.

Skateboard tough — Christopher, Matt. {IL 3-6, -Fic-} — Norwood House Press, 2008, RL 5.5, 167p

Brett's skateboarding abilities dramatically improve after using the Lizard, a skateboard mysteriously unearthed in his front yard, but his friends start to wonder if the skateboard is haunted.

Slam — Hornby, Nick. {IL YA, -Fic-} — Riverhead Trade, RL 4.4, 2008.

At the age of fifteen, Sam Jones's girlfriend gets pregnant and Sam's life of skateboarding and daydreaming about Tony Hawk changes drastically.

Southpaw — Wallace, Rich. {IL 5-8, -Fic-} — Viking, 2006, RL 5.3, 112p

After moving to New Jersey following his parents' divorce, Jimmy Fleming tries out for the seventh-grade baseball team while also trying to cope with his new life and dealing with his overly-competitive father. *(Winning Season, Book 6)*

Sports illustrated kids year in sports 2008 — {IL 5-8, 796} — Scholastic Reference, 2007, RL 6.5, 319p

A sports almanac especially for young fans, providing information and statistics on the 2007 sports season, covering football, baseball, basketball, hockey, soccer, action sports, golf, motor sports, tennis, swimming, track and field, and Olympics.

Take me out to the ballgame: the sensational baseball song — Norworth, Jack. {IL K-3, 796.357} — Little, Brown, 2006, RL 1.7, 32p

The lyrics of the familiar song, illustrated by pictures based on the World Series games played between the Dodgers and the Yankees in 1949 in Ebbets Field.

Teammates — Barber, Tiki. {IL K-3, 796.332} — Simon & Schuster Books for Young Readers, 2006, RL 2.9, 32p

A story of teamwork and perseverance based on the childhoods of National Football League stars and twin brothers Tiki and Ronde Barber.

Twelve rounds to glory: the story of Muhammad Ali — Smith, Charles R. {IL 5-8, 796.83} — Candlewick Press, 2007, RL 7.5, 80p

Rap-inspired verse and illustrations describe the life of Muhammad Ali, discussing his bouts, struggles with societal prejudice, Islamic faith, Olympic glory, and more.

Under the baseball moon — Ritter, John H. {IL 5-8, -Fic-} — Philomel Books, 2006, RL 6.2, 283p

Andy and Glory, two fifteen-year-olds from Ocean Beach, California, pursue their respective dreams of becoming a famous musician and a professional softball player.

The water patrol: saving surfers' lives in big waves — Barr, Linda. {IL 5-8, 797.2} — Red Brick Learning, 2006, RL 2.3, 48p

Describes how water patrol teams help protect surfers who ride the big waves, and examines the training they need. *(High Five Reading series)*

We are the ship: the story of Negro League baseball — Nelson, Kadir. {IL 3-6, 796.357} — Jump at the Sun/Hyperion, 2008, RL 6, 88p

> Explores the history of Negro League baseball teams, discussing owners, players, hardships, wins, and losses; and includes illustrations.

What athletes are made of — Piven, Hanokh. {IL K-3, 796} — Atheneum Books for Young Readers, 2006, RL 3.9, 34p

> Contains brief profiles of great athletes from a wide range of sports, providing information about each one's accomplishments, in simple text with illustrations.

Web Connections

ALA Great Websites: Sports <http://www.ala.org/gwstemplate.cfm?section=greatwebsites&template=/cfapps/gws/displaysection.cfm&sec=10>

The Ancient Olympic Games <http://www.perseus.tufts.edu/Olympics/>

BaseballRox <http://www.baseballrox.com>

Black Baseball's Negro League <http://www.blackbaseball.com/>

Dan Gutman <http://www.dangutman.com/index.html>

Facthound.com Sports <http://facthound.com/Category.aspx?CategoryID=19>

International Tennis Federation <http://www.itftennis.com/>

Judo Information <http://www.JudoInfo.com>

KidsRunning.com < http://www.kidsrunning.com>

Major League Baseball <http://mlb.mlb.com/NASApp/mlb/index.jsp>

Major League Soccer <http://www.mlsnet.com/MLS/index.jsp>

MSNBC Matt Lauer interview with Mike Lupica <http://www.msnbc.msn.com/id/12270717/>

National Baseball Hall of Fame <http://www.baseballhalloffame.org/>

National Basketball Association <http://www.nba.com/>

National Football League <http://www.nfl.com>

National Hockey League <http://www.nhl.com>

Play Sports TV <http://www.playsportstv.com>

Racewalk.com <http://www.racewalk.com/defaultRW.asp>

Special Olympics Public Website <http://www.specialolympics.org/Special+Olympics+Public+Website/default.htm>

Sport Science @ the Exploratorium <http://www.exploratorium.edu/sports/index.html>

Sports Illustrated for Kids <http://www.sikids.com>

Tackle Reading: Games and Activities <http://www.eduplace.com/tacklereading/index.html>

United States Fencing Association <http://www.USFencing.org>

USA Track and Field <http://www.usatf.org>

Vicki Blackwell Teacher Templates <http://www.vickiblackwell.com/ppttemplates.html>

CHAPTER 4

And a Shot Rang Out: Mystery and Adventure

E verybody loves a mystery. We are quickly drawn into the search for clues, throwing or swallowing red herrings along the way. Who hasn't savored the triumphant feeling of "I told you so!" when you have correctly solved the case? Using mysteries to teach reading and writing allows kids the opportunity to use critical thinking skills and utilize higher learning skills. Using material they love just makes our job easier.

Living the life of James Bond is something most guys only dream about. But through the pages of a book, characters like Alex Rider can take us from one nail-biting adventure to another in just the turn of a page. Adventure stories feature characters who take risks. They are brave. They open doors we would run from. They wear us out and keep us reading into the dark of night. They make us read and read more.

Many of the books in this chapter have male leading characters. They are strong guys who live through tough situations. They make bad choices. They trust the wrong person. But in the end, the most important choices they make turn out to be good ones. They live through their adversity. Good guys triumph over evil. The message in these stories may be as important as the action.

Teacher/Librarian Strategies:

- Celebrate Kids Love A Mystery Week in February.

- Create a display of adventure stories in the school library using props from featured books.

- Create a word scramble based on one of the books. See Kidsreads.com for examples or create your own at Discovery School.com <http://puzzlemaker.school.discovery.com/>

- Do a reading rotation. Students choose books, read for 5 minutes and pass it to the person on their right. How many of those books do they want more time to read? Provide them a list of the featured books on a bookmark.

- Have a last sentence contest. Students write the best last sentence from an adventure book that they are reading on a bulletin board. Title it: *And a shot rang out!*

- Have five extra minutes? Play I Spy. Yes, I Spy. Students use clues and the process of elimination to identify what someone is seeing.

- How observant are your kids? After having them work together on an activity for five minutes, have them turn back to back and write a description of what their partner looks like. Give them time to be descriptive.

- Have students write their own adventure stories. See Seven Days of Daring Deeds at the end of this chapter.

- Introduce the genre of mystery by using a short picture book so that it is easier to spot the components. Use Weisner's *Tuesday* or Ruth Brown's *A Dark, Dark Tale,* for example. Weston Woods makes a great video of *Tuesday.*

- Make a bulletin board display with the last sentence of several chapters of these adventure books. Can students guess which sentence came from which book?

- Make a display of mystery books. Use a black cloth as the backdrop; add streamers of Police Line Do Not Cross tape and footprints.

- Make bookmarkers of favorite mystery series for students to use.

- Play 20 questions. Students are again using critical thinking skills and using process of elimination to draw conclusions—the same skills it takes for solving a mystery. Play online at 20Q.com.

- Question of the day: Each day give a new clue to the identity of someone you are studying in a content area. By Friday, students must make a guess and tell why they have chosen this person. Use your databases, like Grolier's Online feature "What happened today" to locate your questions.

- Use board games like Clue during your study of mysteries. It may help kids to think more like a detective.

- Use Mystery Chart at end of chapter to chart plot elements.

- Visit Carol Hurst's website for ideas with older mysteries.

- Write a mystery from a bag. Put several objects in a bag—chewing gum wrapper, toothpick, receipt, etc. Have students write a mystery using the items in the bag. To get them started, you might create a bag using a selection from *Two Minute Mysteries* by Donald Sobol. Read the story and ask students to recall how the bag's items fit into the story.

Books with Mystery and Adventure

Title — Author. {Interest Level, Dewey Decimal Classification} — Publisher, Year, Reading Level, Number of Pages

---

Airman — Colfer, Eoin. {IL 5-8, -Fic-} — Hyperion Books for Children, 2008, RL 7.1, 412p

In the 1890s on an island off the Irish coast, Conor Broekhart is falsely imprisoned and passes the solitary months by scratching designs of flying machines into the walls, including one for a glider with which he dreams of escape.

Alfred Kropp: the seal of Solomon — Yancey, Richard. {IL YA, -Fic-} — Bloomsbury, 2007, 327p

The last descendant of Sir Lancelot, teenage misfit Alfred Kropp is drawn back into the OIPEP to battle a group of demons bent on freeing themselves from the confines of an ancient relic.

Alfred Kropp: the thirteenth skull — Yancey, Richard. {IL YA, -Fic-} — Bloomsbury, 2008, RL 4.6, 297p

> Alfred Kropp faces an unknown enemy that is causing him to question who he can trust and whether or not he will escape this latest adventure with his life.

Ark angel — Horowitz, Anthony. {IL 5-8, -Fic-} — Philomel Books, 2006, RL 5.9, 326p

> After recovering from a near fatal gunshot wound, teenage spy Alex Rider embarks on a new mission to stop a group of eco-terrorists from sabotaging the launch of the first outer space hotel. *(Alex Rider Adventures series)*

> Check out the Alex Rider webpage for links to CIA and CBI, as well as other "highly classified information."

Artemis Fowl: the time paradox — Colfer, Eoin. {IL 5-8, -Fic-} — Hyperion Books for Children, 2008, RL 5.8, 391p

> Artemis' fairy friends help him travel back in time to find a cure for his mother's rare disease which can only be cured by the brain fluid of now-extinct African lemurs, and is shocked to discover that it was actually his younger self who was responsible for bringing about the animal's extinction.

The black book of secrets — Higgins, F. E. {IL YA, -Fic-} — Feiwel and Friends, 2007, RL 5.9, 273p

> When Ludlow Fitch runs away from his thieving parents in the City, he meets up with the mysterious Joe Zabbidou, who calls himself a secret pawnbroker, and who takes Ludlow as an apprentice to record the confessions of the townspeople of Pagus Parvus, where resentments are many and trust is scarce.

Black duck — Lisle, Janet Taylor. {IL 5-8, -Fic-} — Philomel Books, 2006, RL 4.8, 240p

> Years afterwards, Ruben Hart tells the story of how, in 1929 Newport, Rhode Island, his family and his best friend's family were caught up in the violent competition among groups trying to control the local rum-smuggling trade.

Lisle wrote *Black Duck* based on a newspaper article she read about the capture of the real rum-runner, The Black Duck. Have your students read a newspaper article and make a list of questions that remain unanswered. Create a fictional story that combines those questions with the real facts.

The bone magician — Higgins, F. E. {IL YA, -Fic-} — Feiwel and Friends, 2008, RL 6.3, 272p

> With his father, a fugitive, falsely accused of multiple murders and the real serial killer stalking the wretched streets of Urbs Umida, Pin Carpue, a young undertaker's assistant, investigates and finds that all of the victims may have attended the performance of a stage magician who claims to be able to raise corpses and make the dead speak.

The Calder game — Balliett, Blue. {IL 3-6, -Fic-} — Scholastic Press, 2008, RL 5.4, 379p

> When seventh-grader Calder Pillay disappears from a remote English village—along with an Alexander Calder sculpture to which he has felt strangely drawn—his friends Petra and Tommy fly from Chicago to help his father find him.

The death collector — Richards, Justin. {IL YA, -Fic-} — Bloomsbury, 2007, RL 5.5, 320p

> Three teens and a curator of unclassified artifacts at the British Museum match wits with a madman determined to use unorthodox methods to reanimate the dead, both humans and dinosaurs.

Evil genius — Jinks, Catherine. {IL YA, -Fic-} — Harcourt, 2007, RL 4.9, 486p

> Child prodigy Cadel Piggot, an antisocial computer hacker, discovers his true identity when he enrolls as a first-year student at an advanced crime academy.

Found — Haddix, Margaret Peterson. {IL 5-8, -Fic-} — Simon & Schuster Books for Young Readers, 2008, RL 4.8, 314p

> When thirteen-year-olds Jonah and Chip, who are both adopted, learn they were discovered on a plane that appeared out of nowhere, full of babies with no adults on board, they realize that they have uncovered

a mystery involving time travel and two opposing forces, each trying to repair the fabric of time.

> First in a new series, The Missing, students can watch a book trailer of *Found* at the Scholastic website. Have students create their own book trailers, using a multimedia format such as I-Movie or Photo Story.

Genius squad — Jinks, Catherine. {IL YA, -Fic-} — Harcourt, 2008, RL 5.3, 436p

After the Axis Institute is blown up, fifteen-year-old Cadell Piggot is unhappily stuck in foster care with constant police surveillance to protect him from the evil Prosper English until he gets an offer to join a mysterious group called Genius Squad. *(Sequel to Evil Genuis)*

Ghost of Spirit Bear — Mikaelsen, Ben. {IL 5-8, -Fic-} — HarperCollins, 2008, RL 6.5, 154p

Cole Matthews returns to civilization after his year of exile in the Alaskan wilderness and is ready to face high school, but when the school bullies begin to target his friend, Peter, Cole feels his rage once again coming to the surface and worries high school may prove harder to survive than the wilderness.

The Gollywhopper Games — Feldman, Jody. {IL 5-8, -Fic-} — Greenwillow Books, 2008, RL 5.8, 308p

Twelve-year-old Gil Goodson competes against thousands of other children at extraordinary puzzles, stunts, and more in hopes of a fresh start for his family, which has been ostracized since his father was falsely accused of embezzling money from Golly Toy and Game Company.

Gut-eating bugs: maggots reveal the time of death! — Denega, Danielle. {IL 5-8, 614} — Franklin Watts, 2007, RL 5.5, 64p

Profiles real-life cases that have been solved through forensic entomological evidence and explores the career of a forensic entomologist.

This 24/7 Forensic series from Scholastic includes a great deal of support material, including a test to help readers determine if these forensic jobs are right for them.

Hair and fibers — {IL YA, 363} — M.E. Sharpe, 2007, 96p

Examines how forensic scientists gather and use hair and fiber evidence to investigate crimes and presents related case studies as well as key facts. *(Sharpe Focus Forensic Evidence series)*

Mr. Chickee's messy mission — Curtis, Christopher Paul. {IL 3-6, -Fic-} — Wendy Lamb Books, 2007, RL 4.8, 230p

Flint Future Detective Club members Steven Carter and his friends Russell and Richelle follow Russell's dog, Rodney Rodent, into a mural to chase a demonic-looking gnome, only to find the mysterious Mr. Chickee on the other side.

The mysterious Benedict Society — Stewart, Trenton Lee. {IL 3-6, -Fic-} — Little, Brown, 2007, RL 6.4, 485p

After passing a series of mind-bending tests, four children are selected for a secret mission that requires them to go undercover at the Learning Institute for the Very Enlightened, where the only rule is that there are no rules.

The mysterious Benedict Society and the perilous journey — Stewart, Trenton Lee. {IL 3-6, -Fic-} — Little, Brown, 2008, RL 6.8, 440p

Reynie, Kate, Sticky, and Constance, all graduates of the Learning Institute for the Very Enlightened and members of the Benedict Society, embark on a scavenger hunt that turns into a desperate search for the missing Mr. Benedict.

The name of this book is secret — Bosch, Pseudonymous. {IL 3-6, -Fic-} — Little, Brown, 2007, RL 5.7, 360p

Cassandra and Max find a missing magician's notebook and start to investigate the fire which burnt down his house and his mysterious "symphony of smells."

The style of "Bosch's" book is genius. The first chapter is written in x's. Chapter one and a half apologizes for not being able to let us read chapter 1, as it is too secret. The mystery of the mystery is what pulls readers into the story.

The Neddiad: how Neddie took the train, went to Hollywood, and saved civilization — Pinkwater, Daniel Manus. {IL 5-8, -Fic-} — Houghton Mifflin, 2007, RL 5, 307p

When shoelace heir Neddie Wentworthstein and his family take the train from Chicago to Los Angeles in the 1940s, he winds up in possession of a valuable Indian turtle artifact whose owner is supposed to be able to prevent the impending destruction of the world, but he is not sure exactly how.

Ask students to determine the meaning of the subtitle. Write new subtitles for favorite books. It could be a game where other students have to guess the original title.

The postcard — Abbott, Tony. {IL 3-6, -Fic-} — Little, Brown, 2008, RL 4, 358p

Thirteen-year-old Jason finds an old postcard at his recently-deceased grandmother's house that leads him on an adventure blending figures from an old, unfinished detective story with his family's past.

Punished! — Lubar, David. {IL 3-6, -Fic-} — Darby Creek Pub., 2006, RL 3.9, 96p

Logan and his friend Benedict are playing tag in the library when a mysterious man punished him by making him speak only in puns.

Ask students to collect puns to post on the board when reading *Punished!* Did you know? Lubar works on writing video games!

A samurai never fears death: a samurai mystery — Hoobler, Dorothy. {IL 5-8, -Fic-} — Sleuth/Philomel, 2007, RL 6.7, 198p

Returning home to investigate the possible connection of his family's tea shop with smugglers, Seikei, now a samurai in eighteenth-century Japan, becomes involved in a murder at a local puppet theater and saving the life of his sister's accused boyfriend.

The seance — Lawrence, Iain. {IL 3-6, -Fic-} — Delacorte Press, 2008, RL 5.7, 262p

In 1926, magician Harry Houdini arrives in the city to perform magic and to expose fraudulent mediums but thirteen-year-old Scooter King, who works for his mother making her seances seem real, needs Houdini's help to solve a murder.

The seer of shadows — Avi. {IL 3-6, -Fic-} — HarperCollins, 2008, RL 6.1, 202p

Photographer Horace Carpetine is commissioned to do a portrait for society matron Mrs. Frederick Von Macht; however, the photos evoke both the image and the ghost of the Von Macht's dead daughter, Eleanora, who has returned to seek vengeance on those who killed her.

Snakehead — Horowitz, Anthony. {IL 5-8, -Fic-} — Philomel Books, 2007, RL 5.4, 388p

Alex Rider crash lands off the coast of Australia where he is recruited by the Australian Secret Service to infiltrate one of the ruthless gangs operating across South East Asia.

Solving crimes with trace evidence — Jeffrey, Gary. {IL 5-8, 363.25} — Rosen Central, 2008, RL 5.6, 48p

Looks at the techniques investigators use to find and collect trace evidence at crime scenes, and provides graphic novel accounts of famous cases in which trace evidence led to the apprehension of a killer.

Steel Trapp: the challenge — Pearson, Ridley. {IL 5-8, -Fic-} — Disney Editions, 2008, RL 8.1, 324p

On a two-day train trip to enter his invention in the National Science Competition in Washington, D.C., fourteen-year-old Steven "Steel" Trapp, possessor of a remarkable photographic memory, becomes embroiled in an international plot of kidnapping and bribery that may have links to terrorists.

The Titan's curse — Riordan, Rick. {IL 5-8, -Fic-} — Miramax Books/Hyperion Books for Children, 2007, RL 5.3, 312p

The disappearance of the goddess Artemis while out hunting a rare, ancient monster, prompts a group of her followers to join Percy and his friends in an attempt to find and rescue her before the winter solstice, when her influence is needed to sway the Olympian Council regarding the war with the Titans.

Tunnels — Gordon, Roderick. {IL 5-8, -Fic-} — Chicken House/Scholastic, 2008, RL 6.9, 472p

When Will Burrows and his friend Chester embark on a quest to find Will's archaeologist father, who has inexplicably disappeared, they are led to a labyrinthine world underneath London, full of sinister inhabitants with evil intentions toward "Topsoilers" like Will and his father.

The Wright 3 — Balliett, Blue. {IL 5-8, -Fic-} — Scholastic Press, 2006, RL 6.1, 318p

In the midst of a series of unexplained accidents and mysterious coincidences, sixth-graders Calder, Petra, and Tommy lead their classmates in an attempt to keep Frank Lloyd Wright's famous Robie House from being demolished. *(Sequel to Chasing Vermeer)*

> Live near Chicago? You can take a Wright 3 tour of the Robie House.

Web Connections

Alex Rider <http://www.alexrider.com/Home>

Carol Hurst on Mysteries <http://www.carolhurst.com/subjects/mysteries.html>

CIA for Kids <http://www.odci.gov/cia/ciakids/>

Discovery School: Puzzlemaker <http://puzzlemaker.school.discovery. com/>

Edgar Allan Poe Award <http://www.mysterywriters.org/pages/awards/index.htm>

Education World—It's a Mystery, 5 lessons <http://www.education-world.com/a_lesson/lesson299.shtml>

FBI Kids Page (with links to Youth Page Grades 6-12) <http://www.fbi.gov/kids/k5th/kidsk5th.htm>

History Mystery at Scholastic—solve the puzzle about these historic mysteries <http://teacher.scholastic.com/histmyst/index.asp>

Kids Love a Mystery Week <http://www.kidsloveamystery.com/>

KidsReads.com: for Trivia and series information and games <http://www.kidsreads.com/index.asp>

MysteryNet's Kids Mysteries: Stories to Solve, Puzzles and Magic Tricks <http://kids.mysterynet.com/>

NOBLE Children's Library Links to Mystery Pages <http://www.noblenet.org/nobchild/special/mystery.htm>

Robie House <http://www.wrightplus.org/robiehouse/robiehouse.html>

Scholastic.com Mystery Writing with Joan Lowery Nixon <http://teacher.scholastic.com/writewit/mystery/index.htm>

Sir Arthur Conan Doyle official site <http://www.sherlockholmesonline.org/>

Thunk.com to create mystery messages <http://www.thunk.com/index.cgi>

Time Warp Trio Home Page <http://www.timewarptrio.com/>

Figure 2 Mystery Chart

Title	Hero	Sidekick	Villain	Victim	Crime	Location	Solution

Writing Activity

Seven Days of Daring Deeds

Language Arts/Art

Students will write and publish an adventure story in which main events take place on consecutive days of the week.

What You Need

- Computer for each group or you could rotate a group typist to the workstations you do have

- Binding materials (comb-binder, a two-hole punch and yarn, or a stapler)

What to Do

1. Break students into seven groups. Each group will write an adventure for each day of the week—e.g., Group 1 has Sunday, etc. Limit their writing to one or two typed pages.

2. As a class, determine the story's setting, characters, and plot.

   SETTING: As a trip destination, connect your social studies units into possible settings. Remember that time of the year can be very important to the plot. How can season change what happens?

   CHARACTERS: Students decide who the characters are (perhaps a family of three or two friends and a dog) and how the characters are traveling (e.g., on foot, on a subway, in a car, on a plane).

   PLOT: Have students brainstorm some exciting events (a thrilling canoe ride, an encounter with wild animals, a scary climb up a mountain, etc.) to build into their story. List the events on the board.

3. Work with each team as students plan and write the story. Monitor the groups to make sure that they are on the right track. Work with your media specialist for sources to provide content in the stories. *(You can't write about a story that takes place at the beach if you don't know anything about the beach!)*

4. Combine the groups' work. Read the whole story to the class. Talk about transitions from one day to the next. What sentences should be added to make the story flow from one day to next day?

5. Before students publish their book, work with three or four students to finalize the text. Then have students make the final draft.

6. While students are making final corrections, choose a student from each group to illustrate each day's adventure. Illustrations can be computer generated or created by hand.

7. Ask a student to place the illustrations where they belong in the text and then bind the book. Create a title page with verso. Add a dedication.

8. Donate your book to the school library where everyone will be able to read it.

CHAPTER 5

Knock! Knock! Who's There?: Humor

A muffin is in the oven when another muffin is placed in the oven with it. The first muffin says to the new muffin, "It's hot in here, isn't it?" The second muffin screams and shouts, "Oh, my gosh! It's a talking muffin!" (ba-da bump). It's not funny if you have to explain it. Humor is different from person to person. It's certainly different between girls and boys. Mention of body parts, silly puns, and good-natured joking are things that adults may discourage, but boys will laugh and laugh at it. Ask a man and a woman if they think The Three Stooges are funny. Men do; most women don't. Dav Pilkey and Jon Scieszka have a knack for knowing what makes guys laugh. Knowing what makes a boy laugh and letting go of your "standards of literature" will allow your students to find the books that suit them best.

One thing to note about the literature that is available is that there is far more material for students up to grade 6. Relatively few books that are mostly humorous are published for boys in grades 6-12. However, many of the younger age books are still funny to older boys. Try them and see.

Teacher/Librarian Strategies:

- Encourage kids to read joke and riddle books.

- Post a riddle or joke of the day in your classroom or school library. Better yet, ask one of your boys to do it. Yahoo Kids has more than 2000 jokes online.

- Read a humorous book to your students.

- If the author of a book has a website and students have access to a computer, create an online treasure hunt. (Dav Pilkey has a Treasure Hunt at his site.)

- Make sure there are plenty of multiple copies of 818 (that's jokes and riddles) for everyone.

Books with Humor

Title — Author. {Interest Level, Dewey Decimal Classification} — Publisher, Year, Reading Level, Number of Pages

---

Beastly rhymes to read after dark — Sierra, Judy. {IL 3-6, 811} — Random House, 2008, RL 4.3, 25p

A collection of funny rhymes accompanied by gruesome illustrations.

Bow-Wow bugs a bug — Newgarden, Mark. {IL K-3, -E-} — Harcourt, 2007, wordless, 48p

A wordless story in which a small dog grows annoyed by the bug in his environs and sets out on an eventful trek after it, down his street.

Captain Underpants and the invasion of the incredibly naughty cafeteria ladies from outer space (and the subsequent assault of the equally evil lunchroom zombie nerds): the third epic novel — Dav Pilkey. {IL 3-6, -Fic-} — Blue Sky Press, 2008, RL 4.4, 134p

Only Captain Underpants can stop the three evil space aliens who have invaded Jerome Horwitz Elementary School and turned everyone into lunchroom zombie nerds. *(This Collector's Edition includes a CD with songs by Koji Matsumoto and other features.)*

Diary of a wimpy kid: Rodrick rules — Kinney, Jeff. {IL 3-6, -Fic-} — Amulet Books, 2008, RL 6.1, 216p

Greg Heffley tells about his summer vacation and his attempts to steer clear of trouble when he returns to middle school and tries to keep his older brother, Rodrick, from telling everyone about Greg's most humiliating experience of the summer.

Dodger and me — Sonnenblick, Jordan. {IL 3-6, -Fic-} — Feiwel and Friends, 2008, RL 4.3, 171p

Miserable because his only friend moved away and he has once again caused his baseball team to lose a game, fifth-grader Willy Ryan's life suddenly becomes a lot more interesting when he finds Dodger, a furry, blue chimpanzee that only he can see, and he has to decide what he really wishes for in life.

Fly high, Fly Guy! — Arnold, Tedd. {IL K-3, -E-} — Scholastic, 2008, RL 1.2, 30p

When Buzz, his parents, and his pet fly go on a road trip and get lost, Fly Guy comes to the rescue to help them find their way home.

> The Fly Guy series is an award winning (Theodor Geisel honor) book series with several volumes now published.

Frankenstein takes the cake — Rex, Adam. {IL K-3, 811} — Harcourt, 2008, RL 3.2, 39p

Contains poems about the bad habits, anxieties, and other fears and foibles of monsters, including selections about Frankenstein's wedding.

> Have an open mike time for stand-up comedy. Kids can tell jokes and stories at lunch or recess.

Help me, Mr. Mutt!: expert answers for dogs with people problems — Stevens, Janet. {IL K-3, -E-} — Harcourt, 2008, RL 2.3, 50p

Dogs across the United States write to Mr. Mutt, a people expert, for help with their humans.

> Mr. Mutt is the Dear Abby of canines. Have students create their own letters and exchange with each other for letter writing and answering practice.

The incredible book eating boy — Jeffers, Oliver. {IL K-3, -E-} — Philomel Books, 2007, RL 2.2, 32p

Henry loves to eat books, until he begins to feel quite ill and decides that maybe he could do something else with the books he has been devouring.

Knucklehead: tall tales & mostly true stories about growing up Scieszka — Scieszka, Jon. {IL 3-6, 813} — Viking, 2008, RL 4.6, 106p

Presents a memoir of what it was like to grow up in the 1950s and other almost true stories by American children's author Jon Scieszka.

LaRue for mayor: letters from the campaign trail — Teague, Mark. {IL K-3, -E-} — Blue Sky Press, 2008, RL 3, 32p

Mrs. LaRue's dog, Ike, decides to run for mayor of Snort City after realizing the front-runner, Chief Bugwort, wants to enforce leash, curfew, and other laws for dogs.

Never take a shark to the dentist: (and other things not to do) — Barrett, Judi. {IL K-3, -E-} — Atheneum Books for Young Readers, 2008, RL 2, 34p

A list of things one should not do with various animals, such as "hold hands with a lobster."

On top of the potty: and other get-up-and-go songs — Katz, Alan. {IL K-3, 782.42} — Margaret K. McElderry Books, 2008, RL 2.2, 32p

Well-known songs with new lyrics encourage toddlers to trade in their diapers for the potty chair, including "If You Gotta Go Do Poopy," sung to the tune of "If You're Happy and You Know It."

> Either sing the Potty poems with your students or give them the poems and have them try to figure out what song it could be sung to.

The perfect nest — Friend, Catherine. {IL K-3, -E-} — Candlewick Press, 2007, RL 2.3, 34p

> With hopes of making a delicious omelet, Jack the cat builds a nest to catch a chicken, but ends up attracting more than the bird.

Pirates don't change diapers — Long, Melinda. {IL K-3, -E-} — Harcourt, 2007, RL 2.9, 42p

> Braid Beard and his pirate crew return to retrieve the treasure they buried in Jeremy Jacob's backyard, but first they must help calm his baby sister, Bonney Anne, whom they awoke from her nap.

Pirates drive buses — Morgan, Christopher. {IL 3-6, -Fic-} — Roaring Brook Press, 2008, 2007, RL 4.1, 73p

> While conducting a tour of the "landlubbers' world" for a bus load of sea creatures, Pirate intercepts school-bound siblings Billy and Heidi and enlists their aid in recovering his hijacked ship from a troupe of mischievous monkey-crabs. *(Melvin Beederman Superhero, Book 2)*

The retired kid — Agee, Jon. {IL K-3, -E-} — Hyperion Books for Children, 2008, RL 2.6, 32p

> Although he enjoys some aspects of his retirement, eight-year-old Brian gains a new perspective on his job of being a child after spending time in Florida's Happy Sunset Retirement Community.

Scoop!: an exclusive by Monty Molenski — Kelly, John. {IL K-3, -E-} — Candlewick Press, 2007, RL 3.6, 32p

> Reporter Monty Molenski, trying to find his first front page story, decides to investigate his co-workers who he believes are behaving strangely, and in the process accidentally snaps some amazing news photographs.

Sipping spiders through a straw: campfire songs for monsters — DiPucchio, Kelly S. {IL 3-6, 782.42164} — Scholastic Press, 2008, RL 3.2, 32p

> A collection of creepy critters sing their favorite campfire sing-alongs, slightly altered for little monsters.

Go all the way with the Campfire Songs book. Build a fake campfire and sing these poems while eating marshmallows. You will create a memorable literacy experience for your students.

The Willoughbys — Lowry, Lois. {IL 3-6, -Fic-} — Houghton Mifflin, 2008, RL 5.4, 174p

A tongue-in-cheek take on classic themes in children's literature, in which the four Willoughby children set out to become "deserving orphans" after their neglectful parents embark on a treacherous around-the-world adventure, leaving them in the care of an odious nanny.

Web Connections

Andy Griffiths @ Scholastic <http://www.scholastic.com/ andygriffiths/abouttheauthor.htm>

Children's Literature Network for more titles <http://www. childrensliteraturenetwork.org/favorite/favhumor.html>

Dav Pilkey <http://www.pilkey.com/>

KidSpace @ IPL: Jokes and riddles links <http://ipl.si.umich. edu/KidSpace/browse/fun4500>

Yahoo Kids Jokes <http://kids.yahoo.com/jokes>

CHAPTER 6

To Infinity and Beyond: Fantasy and Science Fiction

Fantasy as a genre gained momentum with the arrival of the Harry Potter series. Who would have ever thought that one book could practically put an end to the age-old question: How many pages is it? Kids who like fantasy will read it—sometimes over and over—just because they enjoy it. Hooking a kid on fantasy can also be a step in self selection. If a student chooses a Redwall book and likes it, he can read for a very long time without asking, "What do I read next?" Of course, he may ask which *one* is next, but all he needs to do is go to KidsRead.com or TeenReads.com to determine the order. Which also defeats another obstacle to reluctant readers: They don't like to ask for help. By finding a series or genre that appeals to them, you help them to help themselves.

Teacher/Librarian Strategies:

- Invite students to talk about the book versus the movie.

- One school has a "Knights of the Ring" program, based on the Dungeons and Dragons theme. For details see <http://www.knightsofthering.org>

- Use a Harry Potter theme (or any other series) for programming in the library. Invite students to come dressed as characters.

- Many fantasies are timeless; however, their covers are not. Redesign the covers of unattractive books by creating new ones, complete with summary teaser, and author and/or illustrator information.

- After reading a fantasy or science fiction in class, ask students to predict what will happen in the next book. Save the predictions to read aloud after the next installment arrives. Who was closest to what the author wrote?

- Many teachers use science fiction to teach science—how about an idea along that line?

Fantasy and Science Fiction Books

Title — Author. {Interest Level, Dewey Decimal Classification} — Publisher, Year, Reading Level, Number of Pages

---

666: the number of the beast — {IL YA, -Fic-} — Point, 2007, RL 5.0, 330p

> A collection of eighteen tales of evil, darkness, and beasts written by various authors, including Joyce Carol Oates, Robin Wasserman, and Melissa de la Cruz.

Alcatraz versus the evil Librarians — Sanderson, Brandon. {IL 3-6, -Fic-} — Scholastic, 2007, RL 5.6, 308p

> On his thirteenth birthday, foster child Alcatraz Smedry receives a bag of sand which is immediately stolen by the evil Librarians who are trying to take over the world; and Alcatraz is introduced to his grandfather and his own special talent, and told that he must use it to save civilization.

The alchemyst: the secrets of the immortal Nicholas Flamel — Scott, Michael Dylan. {IL 5-8, -Fic-} — Delacorte Press, 2007, RL 6, 375p

Fifteen-year-old twins, Sophie and Josh, find themselves caught up in the deadly struggle between rival alchemists, Nicholas Flamel and John Dee, over the possession of an ancient book that holds the secret formulas for alchemy and everlasting life.

The battle of the Labyrinth — Riordan, Rick. {IL 5-8, -Fic-} — Hyperion Books for Children, 2008, RL 5.1, 361p

When demonic cheerleaders invade his high school, Percy Jackson hurries to Camp Half Blood, from whence he and his demigod friends set out on a quest through the Labyrinth, while the war between the Olympians and the evil Titan lord Kronos draws near. *(Book 4 of Percy and the Olympians)*

Visit Rick Riordan's website to obtain lesson plans for use with the Percy series. There are also links to mythology websites that you might use with your social studies classes.

Brisingr — Paolini, Christopher. {IL 5-8, -Fic-} — Alfred A. Knopf, 2008, RL 7.8, 784p

Eragon tries to uphold the oath he made to save Katrina from King Galbatorix, while being pulled in different directions by the needs of the Varden, elves, and dwarves—all of whom need his help and strength to overcome the tyranny of the king.

Charlie Bone and the Shadow — Nimmo, Jenny. {IL 3-6, -Fic-} — Orchard Books, 2008, RL 4.9, 429p

Count Harken, who returns to get revenge on the Red King's heirs, begins with Charlie Bone's family, and when Charlie goes on a quest to save his ancestor with his best friend's dog, Runner Bean, the dog gets trapped in Badlock with everybody else. *(Children of the Red King 7)*

The Diamond of Darkhold — DuPrau, Jeanne. {IL 5-8, -Fic-} — Random House, 2008, RL 5.2, 285p

After obtaining an ancient book with only a few pages remaining, Lina and Doon return to Ember seeking the machine described in the

The Hunger Games — Collins, Suzanne. {IL YA, -Fic-} — Scholastic Press, 2008, RL 5.3, 374p

Sixteen-year-old Katniss Everdeen accidentally becomes a contender in the annual Hunger Games, a grave competition hosted by the Capitol where young boys and girls are pitted against one another in a televised fight to the death.

Inkdeath — Funke, Cornelia. {IL 5-8, -Fic-} — Chicken House, 2008, RL 5.9, 683p.

As Bluejay—Mo's fictitious double—tries to keep the Book of Immortality from unraveling, Adderhead kidnaps all the children in the kingdom, and demands that Bluejay either surrender or doom the children to slavery in the silver mines. *(Volume 3 in the Inkheart series)*

The land of the silver apples — Farmer, Nancy. {IL 5-8, -Fic-} — Atheneum Books for Young Readers, 2007, RL 4.8, 496p

After escaping from the Sea of Trolls, the apprentice bard Jack plunges into a new series of adventures, traveling underground to Elfland and uncovering the truth about his little sister Lucy. *(Sequel to Sea of Trolls)*

M is for magic — Gaiman, Neil. {IL 5-8, -Fic-} — HarperCollins, 2007, RL 5.6, 260p

Presents a collection of eleven short science fiction and fantasy stories by American author Neil Gaiman.

Magic in the mirrorstone: tales of fantasy. {IL YA, -Fic-} — Wizards of the Coast, 2008, 295p

Contains fifteen stories of magic for teen readers, featuring selections by a variety of fantasy writers, including Holly Black, Eugie Foster, Gregory Frost, and others.

The magic thief — Prineas, Sarah. {IL 5-8, -Fic-} — HarperCollins, 2008, RL 6.7, 419p

Conn's life is forever changed when he tries to pick the pocket of the wizard Nevery and instead gets a strong jolt of magic, but, instead of punishing the boy, Nevery takes Conn under his wing, teaches him magic, and enlists his help in finding the person responsible for stealing the city's dwindling magic supply.

Nightrise — Horowitz, Anthony. {IL 5-8, -Fic-} — Scholastic Press, 2007, RL 4.9, 365p

> After telepathic twins Jamie and Scott are attacked by the evil Nightrise Corporation, one of them is imprisoned while the other escapes, left to fight with the other three gatekeepers against the evil Old Ones in order to save his sibling and prevent the destruction of humanity.

> Horowitz's Gatekeeper series is a perfect example of how authors vary their style and audience. The Gatekeeper series is for an older audience than the Alex Rider series and may not be appropriate for your elementary school readers.

Oddest of all — Coville, Bruce. {IL YA, -Fic-} — Harcourt, 2008, RL 5.7, 235p

> Contains nine fiction stories by Bruce Coville, telling of frog mutations, child disappearances, ghosts, and other frights and oddities.

Peter and the secret of Rundoon — Barry, Dave. {IL 3-6, -Fic-} — Disney Editions/Hyperion Books for Children, 2007, RL 6.7, 482p

> Fearing that the sinister Lord Ombra was not destroyed, Peter and Molly travel to the land of Rundoon, which is ruled by the evil King Zarboff. *(Sequel to Peter and the Shadow Thieves)*

Physik — Sage, Angie. {IL 3-6, -Fic-} — Katherine Tegen Books, 2007, RL 6.3, 544p

> Pulled through a glass that brings him back in time, Septimus Heap becomes the apprentice of an alchemist. *(Book 3 of Septimus Heap)*

Queste — Sage, Angie. {IL 3-6, -Fic-} — Katherine Tegen Books, 2008, RL 6, 596p

> Septimus must elude the plans of Merrin Meredith and Tertius Fume in order to find the House of Foryx, a place where all Time meets, and secure the release of Nicko and Snorri. *(Book 4 of Septimus Heap)*

Raven rise — MacHale, D. J. {IL 5-8, -Fic-} — Simon & Schuster Books for Young Readers, 2008, RL 4.8, 544p

While Pendragon is trapped on Ibara, Alder returns to Denduron and reluctantly goes into battle again, and other Travelers face obstacles of various sorts, Saint Dane gains the power he seeks on Second Earth and makes his push to destroy and rebuild Halla. *(Book 9 of Pendragon series)*

The restless dead: ten original stories of the supernatural — {IL YA, -Fic-} — Candlewick Press, 2007, RL 5.1, 253p

Contains ten original stories of the supernatural, featuring selections by Holly Black, Libba Bray, Herbie Brennan, Deborah Noyes, Marcus Sedgwick, and others.

Test — Sleator, William. {IL 5-8, -Fic-} — Amulet Books, 2008, RL 5.2, 298p

In the security-obsessed, elitist United States of the near future, where a standardized test determines each person's entire future, a powerful man runs a corrupt empire until seventeen-year-old Ann and other students take the lead in boycotting the test.

The Titan's curse — Riordan, Rick. {IL 5-8, -Fic-} — Miramax Books/Hyperion Books for Children, 2007, RL 5.3, 312p

The disappearance of the goddess Artemis while out hunting a rare, ancient monster, prompts a group of her followers to join Percy and his friends in an attempt to find and rescue her before the winter solstice, when her influence is needed to sway the Olympian Council regarding the war with the Titans. *(Book 3 of Percy and the Olympians)*

The wizard heir — Chima, Cinda Williams. {IL YA, -Fic-} — Hyperion, 2007, RL 5.0, 458p

Sixteen-year-old Seph McCauley is sent to the Havens, a boys' school in Maine, after being kicked out of several private schools for his untrained magical powers; but his headmaster, Gregory Leicester, has his own mysterious agenda when he agrees to help Seth channel his magic.

Web Connections

Bram Stoker Award: From the Horror Writers Association (HWA). Awards for novel, first novel, long fiction, short story, collections, nonfiction and life achievement, specialty press, work for young people <http://www.horror.org/stokers.htm>

Gatekeeper Series @ Scholastic <http://www.scholastic.com/gatekeepers/>

Hugo Awards: Science fiction awards given by the World Science Fiction Society (WSFS). Includes also Gandalf, Campbell and Special Awards. <http://www.wsfs.org/hugos.html>

Mythopoeic Awards: Honors works published within the last three years that make a significant contribution to scholarship about the Inklings and genres of myth and fantasy studies. <http://www.mythsoc.org/awards.html>

Rick Riordan <http://www.rickriordan.com/>

SFWA Nebula Awards: Science fiction awards given by the Science Fiction and Fantasy Writers of America, Inc. <http://www.mythsoc.org/awards.html>

CHAPTER 7

The Way We Were: War and History

Wh
hat is it like to be in a country where there is war in your backyard? What is it like to go to sleep every night afraid and hungry? Books about war help fill in the gaps that experience has not provided us. These books allow students to see the faces of war and put names to them. They can address issues that children don't know how to express: fear for their own safety, confusion about violence, and disagreement about the politics of war by adults. Whether the stories are based on real people or not, reading books about war allows kids to think critically about the world around them—past, present, and, hopefully, learn for our future.

Thanks to curriculum standards, teachers and media specialists have a built-in link to boys—those who are interested in history. Not only are there nonfiction books to supplement our texts, but there are wonderful fiction books as well. Consider supplementing a social studies textbook with one of these and you may reach students you couldn't reach otherwise. For example, you may have a student who is interested in the yellow fever epidemic of 1793, but he only chooses to read nonfiction. You may suggest that he read Jim Murphy's *An*

American Plague, but you could also pair it with Laurie Halse's *Fever, 1793*. Students who have background information can make an easier transition to fiction with similar content. Kathleen Odean has lists of these "teen books in pairs" on her website.

I had a teacher in the 11th grade who told stories—very much like the ones that Kathleen Krull writes now. Suddenly history came to life. (It also saved me when I was babysitting two wild little boys who were mesmerized by stories of John Adams naked in a river with his clothes stolen or how Abe Lincoln carried pajamas in the top of his hat.) Use these books to supplement your curriculum and bring history to life for your students.

Teacher/Librarian Strategies:

- Use picture books for older readers to introduce an historical era. These are shorter books, often recommended for younger readers, but they can be used with older students to bring background information or summarize a time period.

- Ask students to list specific facts from their book. Validate the information from two different sources—one print and one Internet.

- Provide current event magazines for students to read: *Time*, *Newsweek*, and the daily paper.

- Invite a veteran to speak to your students. Don't wait until Memorial Day or Veteran's Day.

- Read newspapers and network stations for online news.

- Read a picture book related to your social studies or science standard.

- Invite students to write interviews for people of history. Instead of writing an essay, students write the interview questions for their person of history. They also write his or her responses. As part of the presentation, they can enlist a partner to actually present the interview or make a video of it to share with the class.

- Play 20 questions. See 20Q.com and play online.

- Have a Hall of Fame. Many details of history center around a person. Why should this person be in the Hall of Fame?

Books of War and History

Title — Author. {Interest Level, Dewey Decimal Classification} — Publisher, Year, Reading Level, Number of Pages

---

1607: a new look at Jamestown — Lange, Karen E. {IL 3-6, 973.2} — National Geographic, 2007, RL 6.6, 48p

> Explores the history of Jamestown, the first permanent English colony in America, established in 1607, looking at what researchers and archaeologists have learned since 1994 through the Jamestown Rediscovery project.

America at war: poems — {IL 3-6, 811.008} — Margaret K. McElderry Books, 2008, RL 4.2, 84p

> A collection of more than fifty poems and paintings that reflect Americans' views on and response to warfare from the American Revolution through the Iraq War.

Attack of the Turtle: a novel — Carlson, Drew. {IL 3-6, -Fic-} — Eerdman's Books for Young Readers, 2007, RL 4, 149p

> During the Revolutionary War, fourteen-year-old Nathan joins forces with his older cousin, the inventor David Bushnell, to secretly build the first submarine used in naval warfare.

Blaze of silver — Grant, K. M. {IL YA, -Fic-} — Walker, 2007, RL 6.3, 261p

> Using principles of their shared Muslim faith to persuade him, an agent of the Old Man of the Mountain convinces Kamil to lead Will and Ellie into a trap, but Kamil repents and seeks a way to save his friends and redeem himself.

Bog child — Dowd, Siobhan. {IL YA, -Fic-} — David Fickling Books, 2008, RL 3.6, 321p

> In 1981, the height of Ireland's "Troubles," eighteen-year-old Fergus is distracted from his upcoming A-level exams by his imprisoned brother's hunger strike, the stress of being a courier for Sinn Fein, and dreams of a murdered girl whose body he discovered in a bog.

The boy who dared — Bartoletti, Susan Campbell. {IL 5-8, -Fic-} — Scholastic Press, 2008, RL 3.8, 202p

In October 1942, seventeen-year-old Helmuth Hubener, imprisoned for distributing anti-Nazi leaflets, recalls his past life and how he came to dedicate himself to bring the truth about Hitler and the war to the German people.

Cracker!: the best dog in Vietnam — Kadohata, Cynthia. {IL 5-8, -Fic-} — Atheneum Books for Young Readers, 2007, RL 5.1, 312p

A young soldier in Vietnam bonds with his bomb-sniffing dog.

Dark dude — Hijuelos, Oscar. {IL YA, -Fic-} — Atheneum Books for Young Readers, 2008, RL 5.6, 439p

In the 1960s, Rico Fuentes, a pale-skinned Cuban American teenager, abandons drug-infested New York City for the picket fence and apple pie world of Wisconsin, only to discover that he still feels like an outsider and that violent and judgmental people can be found even in the wholesome Midwest.

The donkey of Gallipoli: a true story of courage in World War I — Greenwood, Mark. {IL 3-6, 940.4} — Candlewick Press, 2008, RL 5, 32p

Jack, a soldier serving as a stretcher bearer in Gallipoli, Turkey, during World War I, enlists the help of a donkey named Duffy to carry wounded soldiers off the battlefield.

Don't talk to me about the war — Adler, David A. {IL 5-8, -Fic-} — Viking, 2008, RL 6.1, 216p

In 1940, thirteen-year-old Tommy's routine of school, playing stickball in his Bronx, New York, neighborhood, talking with his friend Beth, and listening to Dodgers games on the radio changes as his mother's illness and his increasing awareness of the war in Europe transform his world.

Don't touch my hat! — Rumford, James. {IL K-3, -E-} — Knopf, 2007, RL 3.3, 38p

A sheriff in the Old West fights crime with the help of his lucky ten-gallon hat.

The dragon's child: a story of Angel Island — Yep, Laurence. {IL 3-6, -Fic-} — HarperCollins, 2008, RL 5.7, 133p

Ten-year-old Gim Lew Yep immigrates from China to America with his father, whom Gim barely knows, and fears he will be a disappointment to his family when he arrives at Angel Island.

Duel!: Burr and Hamilton's deadly war of words — Fradin, Dennis B.
{IL 3-6, 973.4} — Walker & Co., 2008, RL 5.7, 36p

Examines the Burr-Hamilton duel which occurred on July 11, 1804, in which vice-president Aaron Burr and the secretary of treasury, Alexander Hamilton, used dueling pistols to settle their political grievances.

Elijah of Buxton — Curtis, Christopher Paul. {IL 3-6, -Fic-} — Scholastic Press, 2007, RL 5.4, 341p

In 1859, eleven-year-old Elijah Freeman, the first free-born child in Buxton, Canada, which is a haven for slaves fleeing the American south, uses his wits and skills to try to bring to justice the lying preacher who has stolen money that was to be used to buy a family's freedom.

> Christopher Paul Curtis' advice to young writers: 1. Write every day. 2. Have fun with your writing. 3. Ignore all rules—well, keep the big ones, but don't be afraid to try something new.

Fartiste — Krull, Kathleen. {IL K-3, -E-} — Simon & Schuster Books for Young Readers, 2008, RL 1.8, 37p

In nineteenth-century France, Joseph Pujol, a little boy who can control his farts, grows up to become Le Petomaine, making audiences laugh at the Moulin Rouge in Paris with his animal noises, songs, and other sounds. Includes facts about Joseph Pujol and life in turn-of-the-century Paris.

The fire of Ares — Ford, Michael. {IL 5-8, -Fic-} — Walker, 2008, RL 6.9, 244p

When slaves rebel in ancient Sparta, twelve-year-old Lysander, guarded by an heirloom amulet, the Fire of Ares, is caught between the Spartan ruling class, with whom he has been training as a warrior since his noble heritage was revealed, and those among whom he was recently laboring as a slave.

Gabriel's journey — Hart, Alison. {IL 5-8, -Fic-} — Peachtree, 2007, RL 5.8, 169p

Thirteen-year-old Gabriel, a former slave, leaves behind his life as a professional jockey and joins his father in the Fifth U.S. Colored Cavalry at Camp Nelson, Kentucky.

Hard gold: the Colorado Gold Rush of 1859 — Avi. {IL 3-6, -Fic-} — Hyperion, 2008, RL 4.0, 229p

Early Whitcomb, whose family's farm in Iowa is failing due to drought, is enticed by his uncle Jesse to go west and dig for gold to help prevent foreclosure, but during their adventure, Jesse gets into trouble, and Early makes hard decisions while trying to find his relative and the riches that lay hidden in the mountains. *(I Witness Novel series)*

Iron thunder: a Civil War novel — Avi. {IL 3-6, -Fic-} — Hyperion Books for Children, 2007, RL 4.3, 203p

After his father dies in the Civil War, thirteen-year-old Tom Carroll takes his place as the head of the family and secures a job at the local ironwork, where he helps build an iron ship for the Union army and has to decide between being loyal to his side or selling secrets about the ship to Confederate spies.

King George: what was his problem?: everything your schoolbooks didn't tell you about the American Revolution — Sheinkin, Steve. {IL 5-8, 973.3} — Roaring Brook Press, 2008, RL 6.5, 195p

Presents an informal history of the American Revolution, covering the Stamp Act, Paul Revere, and the battle of Ticonderoga, and includes extracts from letters, memorable quotes, and line illustrations.

The kingdom on the waves — Anderson, M. T. {IL YA, -Fic-} — Candlewick Press, 2008, RL 8.1, 561p

Octavian, a young African-American, is brought up as part of a science experiment in the years prior to and during the American Revolution.

The Lincolns: a scrapbook look at Abraham and Mary — Fleming, Candace. {IL 5-8, 973.7} — Schwartz & Wade Books, 2008, RL 6.6, 181p

A dual biography of Abraham Lincoln and his wife, Mary, using photographs, letters, engravings, and cartoons to look at their childhoods, courtship, marriage, children, and other joys and traumas of their years together, including their deaths.

On the wings of heroes — Peck, Richard. {IL 5-8, -Fic-} — Dial Books, 2007, RL 5.1, 148p

A boy in Illinois remembers the homefront years of World War II, especially his two heroes—his brother in the Air Force and his father, who fought in the previous war.

One thousand tracings: healing the wounds of World War II — Judge, Lita. {IL 3-6, 940.53} — Hyperion Books for Children, 2007, RL 3.4, 36p

The author relates the story of her grandparents' efforts after World War II to send packages of food, clothing, and shoes to their friends in Germany and others in Europe who suffered from the after-effects of the war.

Reaching out — Jimenez, Francisco. {IL YA, -Fic-} — Houghton Mifflin, 2008, RL 6.1, 196p

The author describes his experiences as a young immigrant pursuing his education during the 1950s and 1960s.

Silent music: a story of Baghdad — Rumford, James. {IL K-3, -E-} — Roaring Brook Press, 2008, RL 5.6, 32p

As bombs and missiles fall on Baghdad in 2003, a young boy uses the art of calligraphy to distance himself from the horror of war.

Sunrise over Fallujah — Myers, Walter Dean. {IL YA, -Fic-} — Scholastic Press, 2008, RL 5.3, 290p

Robin Perry, from Harlem, is sent to Iraq in 2003 as a member of the Civilian Affairs Battalion, and his time there profoundly changes him. *(Sequel to Fallen Angels)*

Tamar — Peet, Mal. {IL YA, -Fic-} — Candlewick Press, 2007, RL 5.1, 424p

In England in 1995, fifteen-year-old Tamar, grief-stricken by the puzzling death of her beloved grandfather, slowly begins to uncover the secrets of his life in the Dutch resistance during the last year of the Nazi occupation of the Netherlands, and the climactic events that forever cast a shadow on his life and that of his family.

War is: soldiers, survivors, and storytellers talk about war — Aronson, Marc. {IL YA, -Fic-} — Candlewick Press, 2008, RL 6.0, 200p

A collection of essays, memoirs, letters, and fiction that present opposing viewpoints on the nature of war by such contributors as Mark Twain, Bob Dylan, and Ernie Pyle.

Web Connections

A Biography of America: Interactive Maps <http://www.learner.org/biographyofamerica/>

EyeWitness to History: Provides eyewitness accounts from primary documents through the eyes of people who lived through it <http://www.eyewitnesstohistory.com/index.html>

The History Channel: Contains speeches and video clips of important moments in history <http://www.historychannel.com/>

Japanese American National Museum <http://www.janm.org/exhibits/breed/title.htm>

Kathleen O'Dean: Look for books in pairs <http://www.kathleenodean.com/>

KidSpace @ IPL (History and People) <http://www.ipl.org/div/KidSpace/browse/owd9000/>

National Council of Social Studies: Annual award for best trade books K-12, membership provides journal with books and activities for teaching <http://www.socialstudies.org/>

Young Peacemakers Club: Designed to promote peace-making skills and provides a list of books, activities, and teacher resources <http://celebratingpeace.com/>

CHAPTER 8

It's a Dude Thing: Male Characters

*C*harlotte's Web, Because of Winn-Dixie, and *Amelia Bedelia* have more than one thing in common. They are all great books, but the main character is not a boy. Kids like to see themselves in books, so providing books for boys that have a boy as a main character is one step in the right direction. Look for books that have strong male characters. Providing books about boys of different cultures is important too. Using these books can also be a tool for teaching tolerance.

As educators, we need to rethink what we read as a class, or what we read aloud. Take time to make sure that several times a year we are reaching all students, of all races and genders. After all, there are just some things that a girl just wouldn't understand! It's a dude thing!

Teacher/Librarian Strategies:

- Alternate read alouds and class assignments to include boy characters.

- Count the number of books in your classroom library that have boys as main characters. Do you need to supplement your collection?

- Make a display of books in the library: It's a Dude Thing. Display books that fill the bill. Better yet—have some of the boys make the selections.

- Booktalk a wide variety of books to allow for choice.

- Use the stickers at GuysRead.com to mark the spines of books or create bookmarkers and stick them out of the top of the books.

- Develop a blog where boys can write about their books. Blogger.com is free and easy to implement.

- Start a books and boys book club. You could call it Breakfast and Boys and meet before school starts. Perhaps you can ask high school students to meet with your elementary students. There may be Rotary Clubs or other community groups who will read with your students. Read the same book or talk about what they are reading.

Books with Male Characters

Title — Author. {Interest Level, Dewey Decimal Classification} — Publisher, Year, Reading Level, Number of Pages

---

The absolutely true diary of a part-time Indian — Alexie, Sherman. {IL YA, -Fic-} — Little, Brown, 2007, RL 4.0, 229p

Budding cartoonist Junior leaves his troubled school on the Spokane Indian Reservation to attend an all-white farm town school where the only other Native American is the school mascot.

Airman — Colfer, Eoin. {IL 5-8, -Fic-} — Hyperion Books for Children, 2008, RL 6.2, 412p

In the 1890s on an island off the Irish coast, Conor Broekhart is falsely imprisoned and passes the solitary months by scratching designs of flying machines into the walls, including one for a glider with which he dreams of escape.

Alcatraz versus the Scrivener's Bones — Sanderson, Brandon. {IL 3-6, -Fic-} — Scholastic Press, 2008, RL 5.3, 322p

Thirteen-year-old Alcatraz Smedry and his companions seek Al's father and grandfather in the Great Library of Alexandria, where they face undead, soul-stealing wraiths called the Curators of Alexandria, and one of the Scrivener's Bones, a part-human, part-machine mercenary.

Alvin Ho: allergic to girls, school, and other scary things — Look, Lenore. {IL 3-6, -Fic-} — Schwartz & Wade Books, 2008, RL 3.9, 172p

A young boy in Concord, Massachusetts, who loves superheroes and comes from a long line of brave Chinese farmer-warriors, wants to make friends, but first he must overcome his fear of everything.

> Welcome Alvin Ho to the land of boy characters. Expect to see more of him, Martin Bridge, Phineas Macguire, and Stink, as more male characters settle into the world of children's literature.

Antsy does time — Shusterman, Neal. {IL YA, -Fic-} — Dutton Children's Books, 2008, RL 5.8, 247p

Fourteen-year-old Anthony "Antsy" Bonano learns about life, death, and a lot more when he tries to help a friend with a terminal illness feel hopeful about the future.

Big plans — Shea, Bob. {IL K-3, -E-} — Hyperion Books for Children, 2008, RL 1.4, 42p

An unrepentant little boy, sent to the corner for bad behavior, thinks about his very big plans for the future.

> *Big Plans*, illustrated by Lane Smith, begs to be read aloud. Younger students will want to repeat the refrain: "big plans, I got big plans, I say."

Bird Lake moon — Henkes, Kevin. {IL 5-8, -Fic-} — Greenwillow Books, 2008, RL 6.6, 179p

Twelve-year-old Mitch, spending the summer with his grandparents at Bird Lake after his parents' separation, becomes friends with ten-year-old Spencer, who has returned with his family to the lake where his little brother drowned years earlier; and as the boys spend time together and their friendship grows, each of them begins to heal.

The chicken dance — Couvillon, Jacques. {IL 5-8, -Fic-} — Bloomsbury Children's, 2007, RL 4.9, 326p

When eleven-year-old Don Schmidt wins a chicken-judging contest in his small town of Horse Island, Louisiana and goes from outcast to instant celebrity, even his neglectful mother occasionally takes notice of him and eventually he discovers some shocking family secrets.

Chicken feathers — Cowley, Joy. {IL 3-6, -Fic-} — Philomel Books, 2008, RL 5.8, 149p

Relates the story of the summer Josh spends while his mother is in the hospital awaiting the birth of his baby sister, and the story of his pet chicken Semolina—who talks, but only to him, and is almost killed by a red fox.

The compound — Bodeen, S. A. {IL YA, -Fic-} — Feiwel and Friends, 2008, RL 4.1, 248p

Fifteen-year-old Eli, locked inside a radiation-proof compound built by his father to keep them safe following a nuclear attack, begins to question his future, as well as his father's grip on sanity as the family's situation steadily disintegrates over the course of six years.

A couple of boys have the best week ever — Frazee, Marla. {IL K-3, -E-} — Harcourt, 2008, RL 2.7, 32p

Friends James and Eamon enjoy a wonderful week at the home of Eamon's grandparents during summer vacation.

Home of the brave — Applegate, Katherine. {IL 5-8, -Fic-} — Feiwel and Friends, 2007, RL 4.3, 249p

Kek, an African refugee, is confronted by many strange things at the Minneapolis home of his aunt and cousin, as well as in his fifth-grade classroom, and longs for his missing mother, but finds comfort in the company of a cow and her owner.

I am not Joey Pigza — Gantos, Jack. {IL 5-8, -Fic-} — Farrar, Straus and Giroux, 2007, RL 6.9, 215p

Joey's father returns, calling himself Charles Heinz and apologizing for his past bad behavior; and he swears that once Joey and his mother change their names and help him fix up the old diner he has bought, their lives will change for the better.

Lawn boy — Paulsen, Gary. {IL YA, -Fic-} — Wendy Lamb Books, 2007, RL 4.3, 88p

Things get out of hand for a twelve-year-old boy when a neighbor convinces him to expand his summer lawn mowing business.

> In addition to reading about strong male characters, boys need to see strong male role models.
>
> - Plan Father and Son Reading events.
> - Invite local male sports celebrities to read to your students.
> - Encourage your male parents/guardians to take their kids to bookstores and libraries.
> - Hold a training session for dads about how to encourage their sons to read more.

Little brother — Doctorow, Cory. {IL YA, -Fic-} — Tor, 2008, RL 5.9, 382p

Interrogated for days by the Department of Homeland Security in the aftermath of a major terrorist attack on San Francisco, California, seventeen-year-old Marcus is released into what is now a police state, and decides to use his expertise in computer hacking to set things right.

The London Eye mystery — Dowd, Siobhan. {IL 3-6, -Fic-} — David Fickling Books, 2008, RL 6.1, 322p

When Ted and Kat's cousin Salim disappears from the London Eye ferris wheel, the two siblings must work together—Ted with his brain that is "wired differently" and impatient Kat—to try to solve the mystery of what happened to Salim.

Lost and found — Clements, Andrew. {IL 3-6, -Fic-} — Atheneum Books for Young Readers, 2008, RL 5.9, 161p

Twin brothers Jay and Ray Grayson learn about friendship, honesty, and themselves after taking advantage of a clerical oversight in which their new school thinks there is only one Grayson boy.

Martin Bridge: in high gear! — Kerrin, Jessica Scott. {IL K-3, -E-} — Kids Can Press, 2008, RL 4, 111p

Martin Bridge and his friends get ready for the science fair, but a classmate refuses to do his part; and Martin gets advice from a grouchy old aunt and learns the importance of helping others.

Masterpiece — Broach, Elise. {IL 5-8, -Fic-} — Holt/Christy Ottaviano Books, 2008, RL 5.4, 292p

After Marvin, a beetle, makes a miniature drawing as an eleventh birthday gift for James, a human with whom he shares a house, the two new friends work together to help recover a Durer drawing stolen from the Metropolitan Museum of Art.

Mexican whiteboy — Pena, Matt de la. {IL YA, -Fic-} — Delacorte Press, 2008, RL 4.3, 249p

Danny, who is tall and skinny but has a talent for pitching a fastball, cannot seem to fit in at school in San Diego, where his Mexican and white heritage causes people to judge him before he even speaks.

Mr. Lincoln's boys: being the mostly true adventures of Abraham Lincoln's trouble-making sons, Tad and Willie — Rabin, Staton. {IL K-3, 973.7} — Viking, 2008, RL 3.8, 36p

An illustrated story recounting the adventures of Abraham Lincoln and his two sons that focuses on the years Lincoln was President.

Nation — Pratchett, Terry. {IL YA, -Fic-} — HarperCollins, 2008, RL 5.2, 367p

A tsunami destroys everything leaving Mau, an island boy, Daphne, an aristocratic English girl, and a small group of refugees responsible for rebuilding their village and their lives.

Night running: how James escaped with the help of his faithful dog — Carbone, Elisa Lynn. {IL 3-6, -E-} — Knopf, 2008, RL 3.3, 32p

A runaway slave makes a daring escape to freedom with the help of his faithful hunting dog, Zeus. Based on the true story of James Smith's journey from Virginia to Ohio in the mid-1800s.

Phineas L. MacGuire...blasts off! — Dowell, Frances O'Roark. {IL 3-6, -Fic-} — Atheneum Books for Young Readers, 2008, RL 4.6, 188p

Hoping to earn money to attend Space Camp, fourth-grade science whiz Phineas MacGuire gets a job as a dog walker, then enlists the aid of his friends Ben and Aretha to help with experiments using the dog's "slobber."

The retired kid — Agee, Jon. {IL K-3, -E-} — Hyperion Books for Children, 2008, RL 2.6, 32p

Although he enjoys some aspects of his retirement, eight-year-old Brian gains a new perspective on his job of being a child after spending time in Florida's Happy Sunset Retirement Community.

Rex Zero and the end of the world — Wynne-Jones, Tim. {IL 3-6, -Fic-} — Melanie Kroupa Books, 2007, RL 5.8, 186p

Eleven-year-old Rex and his family move to Ottawa from Vancouver in the summer of 1962 when it seems everyone is nervous about the possibility of nuclear war between America and Russia, but his thoughts about the possible end of the world take second place to the mystery creature hiding out in the local park.

Rex Zero, king of nothing — Wynne-Jones, Tim. {IL 3-6, -Fic-} — Farrar, Straus and Giroux, 2008, RL 4.6, 217p

Rex-Norton-Norton, an eleven-year-old boy living in Ottawa in 1962, faces several confusing mysteries, including his father's troubling secrets from World War II, the problems of a beautiful but unhappy woman named Natasha, what to do about his mean and vindictive teacher, and whether or not he should even be concerned about such things.

Schooled — Korman, Gordon. {IL 5-8, -Fic-} — Hyperion Books for Children, 2007, RL 4.5, 208p

Cap lives in isolation with his grandmother, a former hippie; but when she falls from a tree and breaks her hip, Cap is sent to a foster home where he has his first experience in a public school.

Use *Schooled* as a Book Club book. Ask participants to come in hippy attire, bring a natural snack and listen to 60's music before discussing the book.

Smiles to go — Spinelli, Jerry. {IL 5-8, -Fic-} — Joanna Cotler Books, 2008, RL 6.9, 248p

Will Tuppence's life has always been ruled by science and common sense but in ninth grade, shaken up by the discovery that protons decay, he begins to see the entire world differently and gains new perspective on his relationships with his little sister and two closest friends.

Stink and the great guinea pig express — McDonald, Megan. {IL K-3, -E-} — Candlewick Press, 2008, RL 2.2, 118p

Stink Moody, friends Webster and Sophie, and Mrs. Birdwistle visit tourist attractions in Virginia as they try to give away 101 guinea pigs rescued from a laboratory, although Stink is very reluctant to relinquish his favorite, Astro.

Stink and the world's worst super-stinky sneakers — McDonald, Megan. {IL K-3, -Fic-} — Candlewick Press, 2007, RL 2, 130p

A class visit to the Gross-Me-Out exhibit at the science museum inspires Stink Moody to create a variety of terrible smells to put on the sneakers he plans to enter in the World's Worst Super-Stinky Sneaker contest.

> *Stink* Teaching Idea: Visit Megan McDonald's website for a link to Stink's own page which features a PDF file of How to Create Your Own Comic. Girls will like the Way-Not-Boring Stuff to Do link.

Web Connections

Andrew Clements <http://www.andrewclements.com/>

Blogger.com: Create your own online discussion <http://www.blogger.com/start>

Edublog: <http://www.edublogs.com/>

Gary Paulsen <http://www.randomhouse.com/features/garypaulsen/>

Gordon Korman <http://gordonkorman.com/>

Guys Read <http://www.guysread.com/>

Megan McDonald: For links to Stink <http://www.judymoody.com/>

Neal Shusterman <http://www.storyman.com/books/index.html>

Word Press: Download software for creating a blog that will allow your students to write online <http://wordpress.org/>

CHAPTER 9

That's Show Business: Books That Have Become Movies

Don't judge a book by its movie. The Kaiser Foundation reports that children ages 2 to 18 spend 6.5 hours daily in front of electronic media. However, students who are reluctant or challenged readers will approach a book with less appreciation and more background knowledge if they have seen the movie prior to reading the book. Students may also be spurred on to read sequels after viewing movies. Encourage your students to spend time with print by sharing these books that have been or are being made into movies. Providing movie-related books may be just the nudge that reluctant readers need.

Teacher/Librarian Strategies:

- Students can choose a book that they think would make a good movie. They will design a poster to advertise the film (see end of chapter for worksheet).

- Students can create a movie preview of their favorite book using PowerPoint. See *Punk Farm* for an example.

- Go to Quia.com and play hangman with books made into movies or use the questions as a five minute group activity.

- Create a display of these movie-books, using an old film projector or 16 mm film as a prop. Ellison has a filmstrip border die cut.

- Read the book. Compare the movie. Use a Venn Diagram to compare.

- Make your comparison more competitive by having one student at a time read out their list of same or different. Students will cross off any item on their list that someone else reads off his/her own. The person who has something left wins!

- Purchase copies of movie-based books.

- Purchase new releases of books with movie covers.

- *Remember that you must meet all fair use guidelines in order to show movies at school.*

Fair Use Guidelines

Fair use guidelines allow you to use a portion of the copyrighted work if your use meets all four of the following guidelines.

1. **The character of the use:** Did you add new meaning or value to the work?

2. **The nature of the work:** Is the work published or unpublished? Is it factual or creative?

3. **The amount used:** Are you using a little, a lot or the whole work? Generally speaking, the more you use, the more likely you are not following fair use guidelines.

4. **The effect of the use on the market:** What would happen if everyone did what you did? Would it have any effect on the sales of the original work?

Copyright Guidelines

The showing of television or movies must meet all four of the following guidelines.

1. **Face-to-face instructional teaching activity:** Does the work support the curriculum? Is the showing of the work in the teacher's lesson plans?

2. **Legally acquired:** Is the copy a pirated work? Was it purchased with public performance rights?

3. **Presented by instructors or students:** Only teachers or students may show video.

4. **Shown in a classroom situation:** Is the work being shown between school hours in a classroom?

TIP: Purchase a public performance license each year. Some schools include the cost in their student fees. Other schools use book fair profit, educational partners, or organization fees to cover the minimal cost of a PPL.

Librarians: Mark your public performance videos or DVDs on the spine to lessen confusion.

Motion Picture Licensing Corporation <http://www.mplc.com>

Movie Licensing USA (lesson plan ideas are also available) <http://www.movlic.com/schools.html>

Books that Have (or Will Have) a Movie

Title — Author. {Interest Level, Dewey Decimal Classification} — Publisher, Year, Reading Level, Number of Pages (*Production company and year of release, if known*)

Alice's adventures in Wonderland: a pop-up adaptation of Lewis Carroll's original tale — Sabuda, Robert. {IL K-3, -Fic-} — Little Simon, 2003, RL 7.4, 12p

The Amulet of Samarkand — Stroud, Jonathan. {IL 5-8, -Fic-} — Hyperion Paperbacks for Children, 2004, 2003, RL 5.5, 462p

The ant bully — Nickle, John. {IL K-3, -E-} — Scholastic, 2006, RL 3.9, 32p *(2006, Warner Brothers)*

The bad beginning — Snicket, Lemony. {IL 5-8, -Fic-} — HarperCollins, 1999, RL 6, 162p

Because of Winn-Dixie — DiCamillo, Kate. {IL 3-6, -Fic-} — Candlewick Press, 2001, 2000, RL 5.8, 182p *(Walden Media)*

The BFG — Dahl, Roald. {IL 3-6, -Fic-} — Puffin Books, 1998, 1982, RL 4.9, 207p

The Borrowers — Norton, Mary. {IL 3-6, -Fic-} — Harcourt, 1998, 1952, RL 5.9, 180p

Bridge to Terabithia — Paterson, Katherine. {IL 5-8, -Fic-} — HarperTrophy, 1987, 1977, RL 6, 163p *(2007, Walden Media)*

Charlie and the chocolate factory — Dahl, Roald. {IL 3-6, -Fic-} — Puffin Books, 1998, RL 5.9, 155p

Charlotte's web — White, E. B. {IL 3-6, -Fic-} — HarperCollins, 1980, 1952, RL 4.4, 184p *(2006, Walden)*

Cirque du freak — Shan, Darren. {IL 5-8, -Fic-} — Little, Brown, 2002, 2000, RL 7.1, 266p

City of the beasts — Allende, Isabel. {IL 5-8, -Fic-} — HarperTrophy, 2004, 2002, RL 6.9, 406p *(Reading Guide at HarperCollins Childrens)*

Curious George — Rey, H. A. {IL K-3, -E-} — Houghton Mifflin, 1969, RL 2.4, 56p

The curious incident of the dog in the night-time — Haddon, Mark. {IL AD, 813} — Vintage Contemporaries, 2004, 2003, 226p

The dark is rising — Cooper, Susan. {IL 5-8, -Fic-} — Aladdin Paperbacks, 1986, 1973, RL 7, 244p *(Walden Media)*

Dragon rider — Funke, Cornelia Caroline. {IL 3-6, -Fic-} — Scholastic, 2004, RL 5.2, 523p

Eragon — Paolini, Christopher. {IL YA, -Fic-} — Knopf, 2005, 2002, RL 5.8, 503p *(2006, 20th Century Fox)*

The extraordinary adventures of Alfred Kropp — Yancey, Richard. {IL YA, -Fic-} — Bloomsbury Pub., 2005, RL 4.9, 339p

Fantastic Mr. Fox — Dahl, Roald. {IL 3-6, -Fic-} — Puffin Books, 1998, 1970, RL 4.9, 81p

The fellowship of the ring: being the first part of The lord of the rings — Tolkien, J. R. R. {IL YA, 823} — Houghton Mifflin, 1994, 1954, RL 6.1, 398p

The field guide — DiTerlizzi, Tony. {IL 3-6, -Fic-} — Simon & Schuster Books for Young Readers, 2003, RL 5.6, 107p

Five children and it — Nesbit, E. {IL 5-8, -Fic-} — Penguin, 2005, 1902, RL 5.7, 207p

Freak the Mighty — Philbrick, W. R. {IL 5-8, -Fic-} — Scholastic Signature, 2001, 1993, RL 6.3, 169p

The giver — Lowry, Lois. {IL 5-8, -Fic-} — Bantam Books, 1999, 1993, RL 6.8, 180p *(Walden Media)*

The golden compass — Pullman, Philip. {IL 5-8, -Fic-} — Knopf, 2002, RL 6.7, 399p <http://www.randomhouse.com/teachers/catalog/display.pperl?isbn=9780375823459&view=tg>

Great expectations — Dickens, Charles. {IL AD, 823} — Penguin, 2003, 514p

Harry Potter and the chamber of secrets — Rowling, J. K. {IL 5-8, -Fic-} — Scholastic, 2000, 1999, RL 7, 341p

Harry Potter and the goblet of fire — Rowling, J. K. {IL 5-8, -Fic-} — Scholastic, 2002, 2000, RL 7.2, 734p

Harry Potter and the half-blood prince — Rowling, J. K. {IL 5-8, -Fic-} — Arthur A. Levine, 2005, RL 7.3, 652p

Harry Potter and the Order of the Phoenix — Rowling, J. K. {IL 5-8, -Fic-} — Scholastic, 2004, 2003, RL 6.9, 870p

Harry Potter and the prisoner of Azkaban — Rowling, J. K. {IL 5-8, -Fic-} — Scholastic, 2001, 1999, RL 6.9, 435p

Harry Potter and the sorcerer's stone — Rowling, J. K. {IL 5-8, -Fic-} — Scholastic, 1999, 1997, RL 5.3, 312p

Holes — Sachar, Louis. {IL 5-8, -Fic-} — Dell Yearling, 2000, 1998, RL 6.5, 233p *(Walden Media)*

Hoot — Hiaasen, Carl. {IL YA, -Fic-} — Alfred A. Knopf, 2004, 2002, RL 6.1, 292p *(2006, New Line)*

How to eat fried worms — Rockwell, Thomas. {IL 3-6, -Fic-} — Bantam Doubleday Dell Books for Young Readers, 1988, 1973, RL 4.2, 115p *(2006, Walden)*

Howl's moving castle — Jones, Diana Wynne. {IL 5-8, -Fic-} — HarperTrophy, 2001, 1986, RL 8.4, 329p

I know what you did last summer — Duncan, Lois. {IL YA, 813} — Bantam Doubleday Dell Books for Young Readers, 1999, 1973, RL 5.8, 199p

The incredible journey — Burnford, Sheila Every. {IL 5-8, -Fic-} — Dell Yearling, 1996, 1960, RL 6.5, 148p

Inkheart — Funke, Cornelia Caroline. {IL 5-8, -Fic-} — Scholastic, 2005, RL 7, 548p <http://www.kidsreads.com/authors/au-funke-cornelia.asp>

James and the giant peach: a children's story — Dahl, Roald. {IL 3-6, -Fic-} — Puffin, 1996, 1961, RL 5.6, 126p

Jumanji — Van Allsburg, Chris. {IL K-3, -E-} — Houghton Mifflin, 1981, RL 4.4, 31p

The lion, the witch, and the wardrobe (Chronicles of Narnia) — Lewis, C. S. {IL 5-8, -Fic-} — HarperCollins, 1994, 1950, RL 5.5, 189p *(Walden Media)*

Lionboy: the chase — Corder, Zizou. {IL 5-8, -Fic-} — Puffin Books, 2005, 2004, RL 7.5, 263p *(2007, Dreamworks)*

Mary Poppins — Travers, P.L. {IL 3-6, -Fic-} — Harcourt, 2006, RL 6.1, 209p

Matilda — Dahl, Roald. {IL 3-6, -Fic-} — Puffin Books, 1998, 1988, RL 5.2, 240p

Millions — Cottrell Boyce, Frank. {IL 3-6, -Fic-} — HarperCollins, 2004, RL 5.7, 247p

Mrs. Frisby and the rats of NIMH — O'Brien, Robert C. {IL 3-6, -Fic-} — Aladdin Paperbacks, 1986, 1971, RL 5.8, 233p

Nim's island — Orr, Wendy. {IL 3-6, -Fic-} — Dell Yearling, 2002, RL 5.1, 125p *(Walden Media)*

Peter Pan — Barrie, J. M. {IL 5-8, -Fic-} — Atheneum Books for Young Readers, 1980, RL 7.2, 200p

The princess bride: S. Morgenstern's classic tale of true love and high adventure: the "good parts" version — Goldman, William. {IL YA, 813} — Ballantine, 1974, RL 5.8, 283p

Punk Farm — Krosoczka, Jarrett. {IL K-3, -E-} — Knopf, 2005, RL 1.6, 30p *(Dreamworks)*. <http://punkfarm.com/>

The reptile room — Snicket, Lemony. {IL 5-8, -Fic-} — HarperCollins, 1999, RL 5, 190p

The return of the king: being the third part of The lord of the rings — Tolkien, J. R. R. {IL YA, 823} — Houghton Mifflin, 1994, 1955, RL 6.2, 405p

Saving Shiloh — Naylor, Phyllis Reynolds. {IL 3-6, -Fic-} — Aladdin Paperbacks, 1999, 1997, RL 5.5, 137p <http://www.simonsays.com/content/book.cfm?sid=183&pid=407981&agid=21>

Shiloh — Naylor, Phyllis Reynolds. {IL 3-6, -Fic-} — Aladdin Paperbacks, 2000, RL 4.4, 137p

Shiloh season — Naylor, Phyllis Reynolds. {IL 3-6, -Fic-} — Aladdin Paperbacks, 1999, 1996, RL 6.8, 120p

Shrek! — Steig, William. {IL K-3, -E-} — Farrar, Straus and Giroux, 1993, 1990, RL 4.4, 30p

Skellig — Almond, David. {IL 3-6, -Fic-} — Dell, 2000, 1998, RL 3.5, 182p <http://www.davidalmond.com/author/qa.html>

Stormbreaker: an Alex Rider adventure — Horowitz, Anthony. {IL 5-8, -Fic-} — Speak, 2004, 2000, RL 8.5, 234p <http://stormbreaker.com/>

> *Stormbreaker* Teaching Idea: Design a piece of equipment for teen spy, Alex Rider. Label your drawing and write a description of what it does.

Stuart Little — White, E. B. {IL 3-6, -Fic-} — HarperCollins, 1999, 1945, RL 5.4, 131p

The Stupids step out — Allard, Harry. {IL K-3, -E-} — Houghton Mifflin, 1974, RL 3.3, 30p

The tale of Despereaux: being the story of a mouse, a princess, some soup, and a spool of thread — DiCamillo, Kate. {IL 3-6, -Fic-} — Candlewick Press, 2006, RL 4.1, 267p

The thief lord — Funke, Cornelia Caroline. {IL 5-8, -Fic-} — Scholastic, 2003, RL 6.8, 349p

The three musketeers — Dumas, Alexandre. {IL 5-8, 843} — Everyman's Library Children's Classics, 1999, RL 7, 712p

Tuck everlasting — Babbitt, Natalie. {IL 5-8, -Fic-} — Farrar Straus and Giroux, 1985, 1975, RL 5.9, 139p

The Twits — Dahl, Roald. {IL 3-6, -Fic-} — Puffin Books, 1998, 1980, RL 5.2, 76p

The two towers: being the second part of The lord of the rings — Tolkien, J. R. R. {IL YA, 823} — Houghton Mifflin, 1994, RL 6.3, 332p

Walk two moons — Creech, Sharon. {IL 5-8, -Fic-} — HarperTrophy, 1996, 1994, RL 6.6, 280p

Walter the farting dog — Kotzwinkle, William. {IL K-3, -E-} — Dutton Children's Books, 2006, RL 3, 32p

The wee free men — Pratchett, Terry. {IL YA, -Fic-} — HarperTrophy, 2004, 2003, RL 5.3, 375p

Where the wild things are — Sendak, Maurice. {IL K-3, -E-} — HarperCollins, 1984, 1963, RL 4.4, 40p

The wide window — Snicket, Lemony. {IL 5-8, -Fic-} — HarperCollins, 2000, RL 6.8, 214p <http://www.lemonysnicket.com/index.cfm>

The witches — Dahl, Roald. {IL 3-6, -Fic-} — Puffin Books, 1998, 1983, RL 5, 206p

The wonderful Wizard of Oz — Baum, L. Frank. {RL 3-6, -Fic-} — HarperCollins, 2000, 1987, RL 4.9, 267p

Do you know: What color are Dorothy's shoes in the first Oz book? How many original Oz books did Baum write? Why is the Emerald City green?

Zathura: a space adventure — Van Allsburg, Chris. {IL K-3, -E-} — Houghton Mifflin, 2002, RL 4.2, 32p <http://www.chrisvanallsburg.com/home.html>

Read the Book, Make a Movie

Your movie production company has just purchased the rights to create a film based on _____. Create a poster that will promote the upcoming movie. Poster may be digitally created.

Include the following elements:

- A tag line (or slogan for the movie)

- Images (pictures of stars and cover of book)

- Title (What is the film called? Will it have the same title as the movie?)

- Cast (Who will play your main characters?)

- Website (What will you call the website?)

- Pre-release Teacher Idea (Design a reproducible activity that teachers can use to promote the movie—a word find, a puzzle, a list of true or false questions.)

- Distributors (Name of company who is releasing the film. Be prepared to tell why you chose this company.)

- Neatness (It should be neat, clear, and easy to read.)

- Oral presentation (This counts twice.)

Each element will count as 10 points, with oral presentation counting twice.

Due _____

Web Connections

Chris Van Allsburg <http://www.chrisvanallsburg.com/home.html>

David Almond <http://www.davidalmond.com/author/qa.html>

HarperCollins Children's (links for kids, parents and teacher/librarians) <http://www.harpercollinschildrens.com/harperchildrens/>

Internet Movie Database (a subscription service with some free information) <http://www.imdb.com/>

Kids @ Random (guides for teachers and librarians) <http://www.randomhouse.com/kids/index.pperl>

Kids Read <http://www.kidsreads.com/authors/au-funke-cornelia.asp>

Lemony Snicket <http://www.lemonysnicket.com/index.cfm>

Parent Center (for reviews about movies) <http://parentcenter.babycenter.com/reviews/recommendedlists/view/79>

Publishers Weekly newsletter Children's Bookshelf <http://www.publishersweekly.com/enewsletter/CA6583170/2788.html>

Punk Farm <http://punkfarm.com/>

Quia <http://www.quia.com/hm/87303.html>

Simonsays.com (teacher's guides) <http://www.simonsays.com/content/book.cfm?sid=183&pid=407981&agid=21>

Stormbreaker <http://stormbreaker.com/>

Walden Media (teacher's guides, etc.) <http://www.walden.com/web/teach/home>

CHAPTER 10

Say It Proud: Read Alouds

No matter what the age, there are books suitable to read aloud. The benefits to reading aloud are numerous. The more words kids hear, the more words they know. The more they see reading as an enjoyable activity, the more they want to do it on their own.

Which leads to a couple of very important rules for reading aloud. The reader must love what he is reading. If you don't like it, neither will they. If you do, they will likely catch your enthusiasm. Secondly, you must be *prepared* to read the selection. That means you read in advance. Not only will that make it a more fluent reading for the students, you are less likely to be caught by surprise at the vocabulary or turn of events in the story. If you have read it ahead, you should read some aloud to see if it works well aloud. Some stories are just too complicated, among other reasons, for reading aloud.

Visit Jim Trelease's website and read some of the articles about reading and writing. Look at his suggestions for titles in his new edition of *The Read Aloud Handbook.*

Teacher/Librarian Strategies:

- Non-series books will "sell" better if students have familiarity with it or the author and illustrator. Introduce that person to them. Where does he live? Look it up on a map.

- Connect read alouds to curriculum standards by making the time to do it—while you are "covering" your material. For example, if your curriculum standard is that all students should develop an understanding of life cycles of organisms, you could read *Tadpole's Promise* by Jeanne Willis. This fictional tale tells a love story of a caterpillar and a tadpole who fall in love and promise to change. In the end, they both change. It's science and story. Stories can complement textbooks which are often out of range of our student's reading level.

- Discuss the read aloud, both before and after. Introduce the story and provide time for students to talk about it—either in groups, pairs, or as an entire class.

- If you are short on time, read some of the story now and the rest later. If it is a good story, students will remember what happened when you pick it up again.

- Reading picture books aloud to older readers makes it safe for them to listen. After awhile, the "baby book" phenomena will disappear, allowing students to feel safe enough to read them without prompting.

- If the reading of a book—especially a longer one—is not working with a class, STOP reading it. Give yourself, and your students, permission to select another choice. Books are like shoes; every one does not fit all. You can do more damage than good by continuing.

- Students need to know you are a reader too. Read from something you are reading at home. Bring in a newspaper article or a magazine. Read a sentence from your current personal reading selection.

- Provide audio books for your students. Listening Library, Recorded Books, and Weston Woods are among the many producers of audio books. Playaways are available from Follett and Recorded Books. These books on tape look like a small ipod and are player and book in one.

- Pace yourself when reading aloud. One of the biggest mistakes is to read too fast.

- You don't have to change your voice for characters. In fact, if you are not good at it, it works against you.

- Don't over-interrupt yourself. Let them think through what you are doing. Explaining things while reading can be distracting.

- Comfort can be a big factor. Rooms that are too hot, readers that are hard to hear, and chairs that are uncomfortable work against the magic of read alouds.

- Some students cannot sit still and listen. Allow them to sit at a table and draw or write. Insisting on absolute stillness and quiet can be impossible to achieve and steal the joy of the reading.

- The above tips apply to guest readers. Whenever possible, allow choice of material and time to pre-read to guest readers. (It doesn't hurt to have heard them before either.)

- Some titles that seem appropriate for K-3 are not really appropriate for kindergarten. I call these books "Don't Shoot from the Hip." When you read these titles to younger students, it may backfire. You can really upset them. However, if you read about a tadpole who falls in love with a caterpillar and later eats her, you have listeners for life if you read it to an older group.

**Don't Shoot from the Hip:
Titles that Don't Always Work**

Where Willy Went

Bear on the Bed

Tadpole's Promise

Whatever

Ugly Fish

The Ravenous Beast

Princess Justina Albertina

Beware of the Frog

Books to Read Aloud

Title — Author. {Interest Level, Dewey Decimal Classification} — Publisher, Year, Reading Level, Number of Pages

---

A beginning, a muddle, and an end: the right way to write writing — Avi. {IL 3-6, -Fic-} — Harcourt, 2008, RL 5, 164p

> Avon the snail wants to become a writer and enlist the help of his friend Edward the ant on a series of adventures involving an anteater, a tree frog, and a hungry fish.

Beware of the frog — Bee, William. {IL K-3, -E-} — Candlewick Press, 2008, RL 2.2, 42p

> Sweet old Mrs. Collywobbles lives on the edge of a big, dark, scary wood, but has a pet frog to protect her from greedy goblins, smelly trolls, and hungry ogres.

Big bug surprise — Gran, Julia. {IL K-3, -E-} — Scholastic Press, 2007, RL 2.3, 32p

> Prunella knows so much about insects that people get bored listening to her talk, but when her classroom fills up with bees during show-and-tell, Prunella saves the day.

Black duck — Lisle, Janet Taylor. {IL 5-8, -Fic-} — Philomel Books, 2006, RL 4.8, 240p

> Years afterwards, Ruben Hart tells the story of how, in 1929 Newport, Rhode Island, his family and his best friend's family were caught up in the violent competition among groups trying to control the local rum-smuggling trade. *(Listen to the ALA Notable Recording by Listening Library)*

The boy who was raised by librarians — Morris, Carla. {IL K-3, -E-} — Peachtree, 2007, RL 5.1, 32p

> Melvin discovers that the public library is the place where he can find just about anything—including three librarians who help in his quest for knowledge.

The end — LaRochelle, David. {IL K-3, -E-} — Arthur A. Levine Books, 2007, RL 3.2, 36p

> When a princess makes some lemonade, she starts a chain of events involving a fire-breathing dragon, one hundred rabbits, a hungry giant, and a handsome knight.

Fabled fourth graders of Aesop Elementary School — Fleming, Candace. {IL 3-6, -Fic-} — Schwartz and Wade Books, 2007, RL 3.9, 186p

An unlikely teacher takes over the disorderly fourth-grade class of Aesop Elementary School with surprising results.

> Great read alouds also make great audio books. Try setting up a listening center. Purchase some Playaways. Build your collection around ALA's new award winning audio book category.
>
> Other listening tips:
>
> - Suggest audio books that match with curriculum
> - Use audio books as shared reading texts
> - Listen to audio books yourself
> - Encourage students to check out audio materials
> - Encourage students to write reviews of audio books.

Harry Potter and the deathly hallows — Rowling, J. K. {IL 5-8, -Fic-} — A. A. Levine, 2007, RL 6.4, 759p

Follows the journey of the series' protagonist Harry Potter as he attempts to bring an end to his archenemy, Lord Voldemort. *(Listen to Award Winning Jim Dale read the final installation of Harry's tale, published by Listening Library.)*

How to save your tail: if you are a rat nabbed by cats who really like stories about magic spoons, wolves with snout-warts, big hairy chimney trolls—and cookies too — Hanson, Mary Elizabeth. {IL 3-6, -Fic-} — Schwartz & Wade Books, 2007, RL 6.9, 93p

Bob the rat is captured by two of the queen's cats and survives by sharing fresh-baked cookies and stories of his ancestors, whose escapades are similar to those of fairy-tale heroes.

I am the messenger — Zusak, Markus. Read by Marc Aden Gray. {IL YA} — Listening Library, 2006.

> After capturing a bank robber, nineteen-year-old cab driver Ed Kennedy begins receiving mysterious messages that direct him to addresses where people need help, and he begins getting over his lifelong feeling of worthlessness.

Into the Woods — Gardner, Lyn. {IL 3-6, -Fic-} — David Fickling Books, 2007, RL 6, 427p

> Pursued by the sinister Dr. DeWilde and his ravenous wolves, three sisters—Storm, the inheritor of a special musical pipe, the elder Aurora, and the baby Any—flee into the woods and begin a treacherous journey filled with many dangers as they try to find a way to defeat their pursuer and keep him from taking the pipe and control of the entire land.

The invention of Hugo Cabret: a novel in words and pictures — Selznick, Brian. {IL 3-6, -Fic-} — Scholastic Press, 2007, RL 6, 533p

> When twelve-year-old Hugo, an orphan living and repairing clocks within the walls of a Paris train station in 1931, meets a mysterious toyseller and his goddaughter, his undercover life and his biggest secret are jeopardized.

> Scholastic Audiobooks has an award winning version of this Caldecott winning story that also comes with a DVD.

Jack Plank tells tales — Babbitt, Natalie. {IL 3-6, -Fic-} — Michael di Capua Books, 2007, RL 3.9, 128p

> Because he is too nice to be a pirate, Jack Plank looks for a new career, but each night he tells tales of why the one job he looked into that day is wrong.

Nightmare at the book fair — Gutman, Dan. {IL 3-6, -Fic-} — Simon & Schuster Books for Young Readers, 2008, RL 3.3, 230p

> On his way to lacrosse tryouts, the president of the PTA asks Trip Dinkelman to help her with the book fair, resulting in Trip sustaining a head injury which causes him temporary amnesia and makes for an interesting journey home.

No talking — Clements, Andrew. {IL 3-6, -Fic-} — Simon & Schuster Books for Young Readers, 2007, RL 6.9, 146p

The noisy fifth grade boys of Laketon Elementary School challenge the equally loud fifth grade girls to a "no talking" contest.

Pirates don't change diapers — Long, Melinda. {IL K-3, -E-} — Harcourt, 2007, RL 2.9, 42p

Braid Beard and his pirate crew return to retrieve the treasure they buried in Jeremy Jacob's backyard, but first they must help calm his baby sister, Bonney Anne, whom they awoke from her nap.

Princess Justina Albertina: a cautionary tale — Davidson, Ellen Dee. {IL K-3, -E-} — Charlesbridge, 2007, RL 2.3, 32p

A spoiled, demanding young princess who sends her nanny to the far corners of the world in search of the perfect pet finally gets exactly what she deserves.

> Share a book with a larger audience by using a document camera or visual presenter. All you need is an LCD projector or some other sort of projection system. You can even connect it to your computer and switch between the two.

Punk Farm on Tour — Janeczka, Jarrett. {IL K-3, -E-} — Knopf, 2008, RL 1.6, 30p

At the end of the day, while Farmer Joe gets ready for bed, his animals tune their instruments to perform in a big concert as a rock band called Punk Farm.

> Help kids really connect with a story by talking about it after the reading or by completing an activity.

Rabbit & Squirrel: a tale of war & peas — LaReau, Kara. {IL K-3, -E-} — Harcourt, 2008, RL 1.8, 32p

Rabbit and Squirrel are neighbors who never even say hello until someone starts damaging their gardens, and then they blame one another and start a fight that continues even after they meet the real culprit.

Samurai shortstop — Gratz, Alan. {IL YA, -Fic-} — Penguin Group, 2006, RL 4.9, 288p

While obtaining a Western education at a prestigious Japanese boarding school in 1890, sixteen-year-old Toyo also receives traditional samurai training which has profound effects on both his baseball game and his relationship with his father.

> Check out *Shortstop* on tape with Listening Library, which won an ALA YA Notable Recording.

Soul eater — Paver, Michelle. {IL 5-8, -Fic-} — Katherine Tegen Books, 2007, RL 4.8, 323p

When his pack-brother, Wolf, is taken by the Soul-Eaters, Torak must brave the wilderness of the Far North and infiltrate their clan to bring him back.

> Check out *Soul Eater* on tape with Recorded Books, which won an ALA YA Notable Recording.

Tom Trueheart and the Land of Dark Stories — Beck, Ian. {IL 3-6, -Fic-} — Greenwillow Books, 2008, 2007, RL 5.5, 369p

Twelve-year-old Tom Trueheart, accompanied by his friend Jollity the crow, must journey to the dangerous Land of Dark Stories to rescue his brothers and their princess brides, and to try to defeat the villainous Ormestone once again.

Wolf! Wolf! — Rocco, John. {IL K-3, -E-} — Hyperion Books for Children, 2007, RL 3.7, 32p

A retelling of the classic tale about the boy who cried wolf, set in ancient China, in which a hungry wolf wonders if the boy is inviting him over for lunch.

Web Connections

ALA Notable Audio Recordings <http://www.ala.org/ala/aboutala/hqops/library/alarecommends/recommendedlistening.cfm>

Jim Trelease <http://www.trelease-on-reading.com/>

Listening Library <http://www.randomhouse.com/audio/listeninglibrary/>

Recorded Books < http://www.recordedbooks.com/>

Weston Woods @ Scholastic Audiobooks <http://teacher.scholastic.com/products/westonwoods/>

APPENDIX 1

Selected Books That Have Worked for Years

Series

K-3

Bad Bear Detectives by Daniel Manus Pinkwater, Houghton Mifflin

Can You See What I See? by Walter Wick, Scholastic

Diary books by Doreen Cronin, Joanna Cotler Books

Epossumondas by Coleen Salley, Harcourt

Fly Guy by Tedd Arnold, Scholastic

Henry and Mudge by Cynthia Rylant, Simon & Schuster Books for Young Readers

I Spy by Jean Marzollo, Scholastic

Martin Bridge by Jessica Scott Kerrin, Kids Can Press

Mercy Watson by Kate DiCamillo, Candlewick Press

Pinky and Rex by James Howe, Aladdin Paperbacks

Stink by Megan McDonald, Candlewick Press

Walter the Farting Dog by William Kotzwinkle, Dutton Children's Books

3-6

Akimbo by Alexander McCall Smith, Bloomsbury Children's Books

Bone by Jeff Smith, Scholastic

Captain Underpants by Dav Pilkey, Scholastic

Charlie Bone by Jenny Nimmo, Orchard Books

Diamond Brothers Mysteries by Anthony Horowitz, Philomel Books

Dork by Gordon Korman, HarperTrophy

Far Flung Adventures by Paul Stewart, David Fickling Books

From the Highly Scientific Notebooks of Phineas L. MacGuire by Frances O'Roark Dowell, Atheneum Books for Young Readers

Golden Hamster Sagas by Dietlof Reiche, Scholastic

Grey Griffins by Derek Benz, Orchard Books

Guardians of Ga'hoole by Kathryn Lasky, Scholastic

Horrible Harry by Suzy Kline, Viking

How to... by Cressida Cowell, Little, Brown

I Wonder Why, Kingfisher

Keys to the Kingdom by Garth Nix, Scholastic

Magic School Bus by Joanna Cole, Scholastic

Magic Tree House by Mary Pope Osborne, Random House

Melvin Beederman Superhero by Greg Trine, Henry Holt

Million Dollar by Dan Gutman, Hyperion Books for Children

Mistmantle Chronicles by Margaret McAllister, Hyperion Books for Children

My Weird School by Dan Gutman, HarperCollins

Never Land Book by Dave Barry, Hyperion Books for Children

On the Run by Gordon Korman, Scholastic

Poppy by Avi, HarperTrophy

Robert by Barbara Seuling, Cricket Books

Rotten School by R. L. Stine, HarperCollins

Rowan of Rin by Emily Rodda, Avon Books

Sardine in Outer Space by Emmanuel Guibert, First Second

Secrets of Dripping Fang by Dan Greenburg, Harcourt

Septimus Heap by Angie Sage, Katherine Tegen Books

Shadow Children by Margaret Peterson Haddix, Simon & Schuster Books for Young Readers

Spiderwick Chronicles by Tony DiTerlizzi, Simon & Schuster Books for Young Readers

Time Warp Trio by Jon Scieszka, Viking

Toad by Morris Gleitzman, Yearling

Underland Chronicles by Suzanne Collins, Scholastic

Weenies by David Lubar, Tor Books

You Wouldn't Want to Be a ... , Scholastic

5-8

Alex Rider by Anthony Horowitz, Philomel Books

Artemis Fowl by Eoin Colfer, Hyperion Paperbacks for Children

Arthur Trilogy by Kevin Crossley-Holland, Scholastic

Bartimaeus Trilogy by Jonathan Stroud, Miramax Books

Baseball Card Adventures by Dan Gutman, HarperCollins

Books of Ember by Jeanne DuPrau, Random House

Children of the Lamp by Philip Kerr, Orchard Books

Cirque du Freak by Darren Shan, Little, Brown

Cronos Chronicles by Anne Ursu, Atheneum Books for Young

Dark Ground Trilogy by Gillian Cross, Dutton Children's Books

Edge Chronicles by Paul Stewart, David Fickling Books

Fire Thief Trilogy by Terry Deary, Kingfisher

Five Ancestors by Jeff Stone, Random House

Grail Quest by Laura Anne Gilman, HarperCollins

Great Tree of Avalon by T. A. Barron, Philomel Books

Harry Potter by J. K. Rowling, Scholastic

Hermux Tantamoq Adventures by Michael Hoeye, G.P. Putnam's Sons

His Dark Materials by Philip Pullman, Knopf

Inkheart by Cornelia Funke, Scholastic

Joey Pigza by Jack Gantos, Farrar, Straus and Giroux

Kingfisher Knowledge, Kingfisher

Last Apprentice by Joseph Delaney, Greenwillow Books

Lives of the ... by Kathleen Krull, Harcourt Brace

Measle and the ... by Ian Ogilvy, HarperCollins

Monster Blood Tattoo by D. M. Cornish, Putnam

Montmorency by Eleanor Updale, Scholastic

Pendragon by D. J. MacHale, Simon & Schuster

Percy and the Olympians by Rick Riordan, Disney Hyperion

Ranger's Apprentice by John Flanagan, Philomel Books

Raven's Gate by Anthony Horowitz, Scholastic

Redwall by Brian Jacques, Philomel Books

Regarding the ... by Kate Klise, Harcourt

Series of Unfortunate Events by Lemony Snicket, HarperCollins

Squire's Tales by Gerald Morris, Houghton Mifflin

Tiger's Apprentice by Laurence Yep, HarperCollins

Warriors by Erin Hunter, HarperCollins

Winning Season by Rich Wallace, Viking

Young Wizards by Diane Duane, Harcourt

YA

Alfred Kropp by Rick Yancey, Bloomsbury

The Chronicles of Chrestomanci by Diana Wynne Jones, EOS

De Granville Trilogy by K. M. Grant, Walker

Demonata by Darren Shan, Little, Brown

Inheritance by Christopher Paolini, Knopf

Maximum Ride by James Patterson, Little, Brown

Noble Warriors by William Nicholson, Graphia

Pagan Chronicles by Catherine Jinks, Candlewick Press

Wing Books by Kenneth Oppel, EOS

Selected Titles That Have Worked for Years

(See other works by the same authors)

Title — Author. {Interest Level, Dewey Decimal Classification} — Publisher, Year, Reading Level, Number of Pages

---

10,000 days of thunder: a history of the Vietnam War — Caputo, Philip. {IL 5-8, 959.704} — Atheneum Books for Young Readers, 2005, RL 8.9, 128p

The adventures of the dish and the spoon — Grey, Mini. {IL K-3, -E-} — Knopf, 2006, RL 2.3, 32p

All that remains — Brooks, Bruce. {IL YA, -Fic-} — Simon Pulse, 2002, 2001, RL 5.5, 168p

The amazing life of birds: (the twenty-day puberty journal of Duane Homer Leech) — Paulsen, Gary. {IL YA, -Fic-} — Wendy Lamb Books, 2006, RL 4.6, 84p

American born Chinese — Yang, Gene Luen. {IL YA, 741.5} — First Second, 2006, RL 3.3, 233p

The American story: 100 true tales from American history — Armstrong, Jennifer. {IL 3-6, 973} — Knopf, 2006, RL 6.4, 358p

Awful Ogre's awful day — Prelutsky, Jack. {IL K-3, 811} — Greenwillow Books, 2001, RL 3.7, 39p

Black duck — Lisle, Janet Taylor. {IL 5-8, -Fic-} — Sleuth/Philomel, 2006, RL 5, 252p

The book of story beginnings — Kladstrup, Kristin. {IL 5-8, -Fic-} — Candlewick Press, 2006, RL 4.5, 360p

The book thief — Zusak, Markus. {IL YA, -Fic-} — Knopf, 2006, RL 5.1, 552p

Born to rock — Korman, Gordon. {IL YA, -Fic-} — Hyperion, 2006, RL 5.3, 261p

The boy who cried wolf — Hennessy, B. G. {IL K-3, 398.2} — Simon & Schuster Books for Young Readers, 2006, RL 2, 32p

Brothers — Yin. {IL 3-6, -Fic-} — Philomel Books, 2006, RL 3.5, 32p

Burps, boogers, and bad breath — Conrad, David. {IL K-3, 612} — Compass Point Books, 2002, RL 2.3, 24p

Bury the dead: tombs, corpses, mummies, skeletons, & rituals — Sloan, Christopher. {IL 5-8, 393} — National Geographic, 2002, RL 7.2, 64p

Caught by the sea: my life on boats — Paulsen, Gary. {IL 5-8, 818} — Dell Laurel-Leaf, 2003, 2001, RL 7.8, 103p

Chew on this: everything you don't want to know about fast food — Schlosser, Eric. {IL 5-8, 394.1} — Houghton Mifflin, 2006, RL 7.4, 318p

Circle of doom — Kennemore, Tim. {IL 3-6, -Fic-} — Farrar, Straus and Giroux, 2003, 2001, RL 5.8, 203p

City of the beasts — Allende, Isabel. {IL 5-8, -Fic-} — HarperTrophy, 2004, 2002, RL 6.9, 406p

Corpses, coffins, and crypts: a history of burial — Colman, Penny. {IL 5-8, 393} — Henry Holt, 1997, RL 6.5, 212p

Dead man's gold and other stories — Yee, Paul. {IL 5-8, -Fic-} — Douglas & McIntyre, 2002, RL 6.2, 112p

Escape!: the story of the great Houdini — Fleischman, Sid. {IL 5-8, 793.8} — Greenwillow Books, 2006, RL 6.6, 210p

Fantastic beasts and where to find them — Rowling, J. K. {IL 5-8, 823} — Arthur A. Levine Books, 2001, RL 6.9, 42p

Feed — Anderson, M. T. {IL YA, -Fic-} — Candlewick Press, 2004, 2002, RL 4.4, 299p

Fire and wings: dragon tales from East and West — {IL 3-6, -Fic-} — Cricket Books, 2002, RL 5.8, 146p

The frogs wore red suspenders — Prelutsky, Jack. {IL K-3, 811} — Greenwillow, 2002, RL 3.7, 63p

Ghost town: seven ghostly stories — Nixon, Joan Lowery. {IL 3-6, -Fic-} — Delacorte, 2000, RL 5.4, 147p

Gold dust — Lynch, Chris. {IL 5-8, -Fic-} — HarperTrophy, 2002, 2000, RL 6.2, 196p

Good boy, Fergus! — Shannon, David. {IL K-3, -E-} — Blue Sky Press, 2006, RL 1.3, 32p

The gospel according to Larry — Tashjian, Janet. {IL YA, -Fic-} — Dell Laurel-Leaf, 2003, 2001, RL 5.6, 227p

Guts: the true stories behind Hatchet and the Brian books — Paulsen, Gary. {IL 5-8, 813} — Delacorte Press, 2001, RL 5.4, 148p

Handbook for boys: a novel — Myers, Walter Dean. {IL 5-8, -Fic-} — HarperTrophy, 2003, 2002, RL 6.8, 211p

Heat — Lupica, Mike. {IL 5-8, -Fic-} — Philomel Books, 2006, RL 5.6, 220p

The hero's trail: a guide for a heroic life — Barron, T. A. {IL 3-6, 170} — Philomel Books, 2002, RL 6.8, 131p

Hole in my life — Gantos, Jack. {IL YA, 813} — Farrar, Straus and Giroux, 2004, 2002, RL 5.2, 199p

Holes — Sachar, Louis. {IL 5-8, -Fic-} — Dell Yearling, 2000, 1998, RL 6.5, 233p

Home of the Braves — Klass, David. {IL YA, -Fic-} — Farrar, Straus and Giroux, 2002, RL 3.5, 312p

Hoot — Hiaasen, Carl. {IL YA, -Fic-} — Alfred A. Knopf, 2002, RL 5.2, 292p

Isaac Newton — Krull, Kathleen. {IL 5-8, 530} — Viking, 2006, RL 7.3, 126p

John, Paul, George, & Ben — Smith, Lane. {IL K-3, -E-} — Hyperion Books for Children, 2006, RL 3.5, 40p

The journal of Augustus Pelletier: the Lewis and Clark expedition — Lasky, Kathryn. {IL 5-8, -Fic-} — Scholastic, 2000, RL 5.1, 171p

The journal of Biddy Owens: the Negro leagues — Myers, Walter Dean. {IL 5-8, -Fic-} — Scholastic, 2001, RL 6.2, 139p

The journal of Jedediah Barstow: an emigrant on the Oregon Trail —
Levine, Ellen. {IL 5-8, -Fic-} — Scholastic, 2002, RL 7.3, 172p

The journal of Jesse Smoke: a Cherokee boy — Bruchac, Joseph. {IL 5-8,
-Fic-} — Scholastic, 2001, RL 7.9, 203p

The journal of Patrick Seamus Flaherty, United States Marine Corps —
White, Ellen Emerson. {IL 5-8, -Fic-} — Scholastic, 2002, RL 5.3, 188p

Jurassic poop: what dinosaurs (and others) left behind — Berkowitz,
Jacob. {IL 3-6, 560} — Kids Can Press, 2006, RL 5.2, 40p

*The kid who invented the trampoline: more surprising stories about
inventions* — Wulffson, Don L. {IL 3-6, 609} — Dutton Children's
Books, 2001, RL 6.7, 120p

Kit's wilderness — Almond, David. {IL YA, -Fic-} — Delacorte Press,
2000, RL 4.2, 229p

Kokopelli's flute — Hobbs, Will. {IL 5-8, -Fic-} — Aladdin Paperbacks,
2005, 1995, RL 6.5, 148p

Lemony Snicket: the unauthorized autobiography — Snicket, Lemony.
{IL 5-8, -Fic-} — HarperCollins, 2002, RL 7.1, 212p

Leo Cockroach: toy tester — O'Malley, Kevin. {IL K-3, -E-} — Walker,
2001, 1999, RL 4.3, 32p

Loser — Spinelli, Jerry. {IL 3-6, -Fic-} — HarperTrophy, 2003, 2002,
RL 5.2, 218p

More parts — Arnold, Tedd. {IL K-3, -E-} — Puffin Books, 2003, 2001,
RL 2, 32p

Mortal engines: a novel — Reeve, Philip. {IL YA, -Fic-} — EOS, 2004,
2001, RL 6.1, 373p

My father, the dog — Bluemle, Elizabeth. {IL K-3, -E-} — Candlewick
Press, 2006, RL 2.4, 24p

Nailed — Jones, Patrick. {IL YA, -Fic-} — Walker, 2006, RL 5.6, 216p

No more dead dogs — Korman, Gordon. {IL 3-6, -Fic-} — Hyperion
Paperbacks for Children, 2002, 2000, RL 5.3, 180p

Oh, rats!: the story of rats and people — Marrin, Albert. {IL 5-8, 599.35}
— Dutton Children's Books, 2006, RL 5.1, 48p

Oh, yuck!: the encyclopedia of everything nasty — Masoff, Joy. {IL 3-6, 031.02} — Workman, 2000, RL 5.2, 212p

Once upon a tomb: gravely humorous verses — Lewis, J. Patrick. {IL K-3, 811} — Candlewick Press, 2006, RL 3, 26p

Patrol: an American soldier in Vietnam — Myers, Walter Dean. {IL 3-6, -Fic-} — HarperCollins, 2002, RL 4.2, 34p

Phineas Gage: a gruesome but true story about brain science — Fleischman, John. {IL 5-8, 362.1} — Houghton Mifflin, 2002, RL 7.6, 86p

Punished! — Lubar, David. {IL K-3, -Fic-} — Darby Creek Pub., 2006, RL 3.9, 96p

Rats — Zindel, Paul. {IL 5-8, -Fic-} — Hyperion Paperbacks, 2000, 1999, RL 5, 204p

Saint Iggy — Going, K. L. {IL YA, -Fic-} — Harcourt, 2006, RL 5.2, 260p

Samurai shortstop — Gratz, Alan. {IL YA, -Fic-} — Dial Books, 2006, RL 4.9, 280p

Seven wonders of the ancient world — Curlee, Lynn. {IL 3-6, 709} — Atheneum Books for Young Readers, 2002, RL 5.6, 33p

Smart feller, fart smeller, and other Spoonerisms — Agee, Jon. {IL 3-6, 793.734} — Michael Di Capua Books/Hyperion Books, 2006, RL 4.8, 64p

Son of the mob — Korman, Gordon. {IL YA, -Fic-} — Hyperion Paperbacks, 2004, 2002, RL 6.9, 262p

The spider and the fly — Howitt, Mary Botham. {IL K-3, 821} — Simon & Schuster Books for Young Readers, 2002, RL 5.2, 36p

Stop the train!: a novel — McCaughrean, Geraldine. {IL 5-8, -Fic-} — HarperTrophy, 2005, 2001, RL 6.2, 367p

Sumo mouse — Wisniewski, David. {IL K-3, -E-} — Chronicle Books, 2002, RL 3.8, 26p

Tangerine — Bloor, Edward. {IL YA, -Fic-} — Scholastic Signature, 2001, 1997, RL 5.8, 294p

Touching Spirit Bear — Mikaelsen, Ben. {IL 5-8, -Fic-} — HarperTrophy, 2005, 2001, RL 6.7, 289p

Whale talk — Crutcher, Chris. {IL YA, -Fic-} — Dell Laurel-Leaf, 2002, 2001, RL 6.6, 220p

What you never knew about fingers, forks, & chopsticks — Lauber, Patricia. {IL 3-6, 394.1} — Simon & Schuster Books for Young Readers, 1999, RL 5, 30p

What you never knew about tubs, toilets, & showers — Lauber, Patricia. {IL K-3, 391.6} — Simon & Schuster Books for Young Readers, 2001, RL 4.5, 32p

Whatcha mean, what's a zine?: the art of making zines and mini comics — Todd, Mark. {IL YA, 070.5} — Graphia, 2006, RL 5.8, 110p

Wild Man Island — Hobbs, Will. {IL 5-8, -Fic-} — HarperTrophy, 2003, 2002, RL 7.1, 184p

With a little luck: surprising stories of amazing discoveries — Fradin, Dennis B. {IL 5-8, 509} — Dutton Children's Books, 2006, RL 7.2, 183p

The Wright 3 — Balliett, Blue. {IL 5-8, -Fic-} — Scholastic Press, 2006, RL 5.7, 318p

The younger brother's survival guide: by Matt — Kopelke, Lisa. {IL K-3, -E-} — Simon & Schuster Books for Young Readers, 2006, RL 2.7, 32p

APPENDIX 2

Professional Books

Title — Author. {Interest Level, Dewey Decimal Classification} — Publisher, Year, Number of Pages

Action strategies for deepening comprehension — Wilhelm, Jeffrey D. {IL PF, 372.42} — Scholastic, 2002, 192p

> Invites teachers to explore the question of whether or not they are good motivators, explains the theory behind enactment strategies, and describes techniques that may be used in the classroom to promote better reading comprehension.

Best books for kids who (think they) hate to read: 125 books that will turn any kid into a lifelong reader — Backes, Laura. {IL AD, 028.5} — Prima Pub., 2001, 388p

> Profiles 125 books that can help children who normally hate to read learn to love books.

Beyond words: picture books for older readers and writers — {IL PF, 028.5} — Heinemann, 1992, 142p

> A collection of essays explores the wealth of picture books for older readers and writers.

Big ideas in small packages: using picture books with older readers — Pearson, Molly Blake. {IL PF, 011.62} — Linworth, 2005, 116p

> Explains the benefits of using picture books to promote reading and critical thinking in students in grades four through twelve.

Boys and literacy: practical strategies for librarians, teachers, and parents — Knowles, Elizabeth. {IL PF, 028.5} — Libraries Unlimited, 2005, 164p

> Offers strategies for librarians, teachers, and parents to help develop literacy in boys, and focuses on the particular genres that interest them such as adventure, science fiction, fantasy, and mysteries.

Collaborating to meet standards: teacher/librarian partnerships for 7-12
— Buzzeo, Toni. {IL PF, 027.8} — Linworth, 2002, 214p

Reviews the history of cooperation and collaboration in school
libraries since the 1990s, discussing the benefits of collaboration
between library media specialists and teachers at the junior and high
school level; and features a common template for use in planning
collaborative units, as well as a selection of units contributed by teams
across the U.S.

Collaborating to meet standards: teacher/librarian partnerships for K-6
— Buzzeo, Toni. {IL PF, 027.8} — Linworth, 2002, 216p

Reviews the history of cooperation and collaboration in school libraries
since the 1990s, discussing the benefits of collaboration between library
media specialists and teachers at the elementary level; and features a
common template for use in planning collaborative units, as well as a
selection of units contributed by teams across the U.S.

*Collaborative library lessons for the primary grades: linking research
skills to curriculum standards* — Copeland, Brenda S. {IL PF, 028.5} —
Libraries Unlimited, 2004, 158p

Contains seven lessons plans designed for teachers of primary grades
to use in cooperation with school librarians to teach library research
skills in conjunction with science and social studies instruction.

Connecting boys with books: what libraries can do — Sullivan, Michael.
{IL PF, 028.5} — American Library Association, 2003, 121p

Provides librarians, school library media specialists, and educators
with strategies needed to help overcome cultural and developmental
challenges, stereotypes, and lack of role models that can prevent boys
from using libraries.

Curriculum connections: picture books in grades 3 and up — Hurst, Carol
Otis, et al. {IL PF, 372.13} — Linworth Pub., 1999, 278p

Profiles a variety of picture books that are suitable for students in grade
three and higher; includes a summary of the book, information about the
art, and suggestions on how to apply the book to classroom curriculum.

Even hockey players read: boys, literacy, and learning — Booth, David.
{IL PF, 372.42} — Pembroke Publishers Ltd., 2002, 135p

A comprehensive overview of the challenging issues around boys and
reading and writing that includes questions, strategies, and practical
solutions designed to help boys develop their literacy potential.

Going with the flow: how to engage boys (and girls) in their literacy learning — Smith, Michael W. {IL PF, 371.8235} — Heinemann, 2006, 185p

Offers practical suggestions to help adolescent boys and girls build stronger literacy habits, with classroom-test units, lessons, and activities that help keep students involved and interested in literacy learning.

Gotcha covered!: more nonfiction booktalks to get kids excited about reading — Baxter, Kathleen A. {IL PF, 028.5} — Libraries Unlimited, 2005, 219p

Presents over three hundred booktalks designed to help teachers increase their students' interest in reading nonfiction books, arranged thematically in seven categories, including world war; dreamers, flyers, and innovators; and playing with words.

Gotcha for guys!: nonfiction books to get boys excited about reading — Baxter, Kathleen A. {IL PF, 028.5} — Libraries Unlimited, 2007, 269p

Provides bibliographic information for over 1,100 books selected to interest boys in reading, providing annotations for many, and includes several booktalks.

Gotcha!: nonfiction booktalks to get kids excited about reading — Baxter, Kathleen A. {IL PF, 028.1} — Libraries Unlimited, 1999, 183p

Presents more than 350 thematically arranged booktalks designed to help teachers increase their students' interest in reading nonfiction books.

Great books about things kids love: more than 750 recommended books for children 3 to 14 — Odean, Kathleen. {IL AD, 011.62} — Ballantine Books, 2001, 439p

Provides bibliographical information about more than 750 books for children ages three to fourteen.

Great books for boys: more than 600 books for boys 2 to 14 — Odean, Kathleen. {IL AD, 028.1} — Ballantine Books, 1998, 384p

Presents short summaries on more than six hundred fiction, nonfiction, and biography books separated into sections for beginning, middle, and older readers.

How to get your child to love reading — Codell, Esme Raji. {IL AD, 028.5} — Algonquin Books of Chapel Hill, 2003, 531p

Presents guidance for parents on reading aloud, encouraging reluctant readers, rewarding progress, and getting involved in a child's school, and lists over three thousand children's books, providing at-home story-time, craft, cooking, science, and related-reading activities.

I read it, but I don't get it: comprehension strategies for adolescent readers — Tovani, Cris. {IL PF, 428.4} — Stenhouse Publishers, 2000, 140p

The author, a reading specialist, shares some of the problems she has faced in her own classroom; explains how she addressed the dilemma, focusing on what good readers do to make sense of text; and offers suggestions teachers can use to make content more accessible.

Igniting the spark: library programs that inspire high school patrons — Leslie, Roger. {IL PF, 027.8} — Libraries Unlimited, 2001, 172p

Offers detailed information on how to plan, execute, and assess school library programs, discusses the benefits of such programs, and shares winning program ideas developed and carried out by high school media specialists across the U.S.

Linking picture books to standards — Copeland, Brenda S. {IL PF, 372.133} — Libraries Unlimited, 2003, 173p

Contains more than thirty ready-to-use lesson plans for primary school teachers that connect picture books to the national language arts standards of the NCTE and IRA.

Picture books by Latino writers: a guide for librarians, teachers, parents, and students — York, Sherry. {IL PF, 810.8} — Linworth Pub., 2002, 116p

A guide for librarians, teachers, parents, and students that provides information on more than sixty-five picture books by Latino writers; includes brief biographical sketches of each of the authors.

Picture-perfect science lessons: using children's books to guide inquiry, grades 3-6 — Ansberry, Karen Rohrich. {IL PF, 372.35} — NSTA Press, 2005, 304p

Presents a collection of fifteen lesson plans for the third through sixth-grade science classroom that use children's books to help develop interest in science, and contains reproducible student pages and assessments.

The read aloud handbook, Sixth Edition — Trelease, Jim. {IL PF, 372.45} — Penguin, 2006, 340p

Read! perform! learn!: 10 reader's theater programs for literary enhancement — Buzzeo, Toni. {IL PF, 808} — Upstart Books, 2006, 128p

Offers library media specialists, children's librarians, and classroom teachers a wide range of ideas for extending the use of books into content areas through performances.

"Reading don't fix no Chevys": literacy in the lives of young men — Smith, Michael W. {IL PF, 371.8235} — Heinemann, 2002, 224p

Draws from interviews with forty-nine male middle and high school students to explain what motivates adolescent boys and young men to read, presenting suggestions for improving literacy instruction.

The standards-based integrated library: a collaborative approach for aligning the library program with the classroom curriculum — Miller, Donna P. {IL PF, 027.8} — Linworth Pub., 2004, 129p

Explains how teachers and library media specialists can work together to build library collections that complement curriculum and incorporate standards.

Teach writing to older readers using picture books: every picture tells a story — Heitman, Jane. {IL PF, 808} — Linworth Pub., 2004, 143p

Presents more than one hundred standards-based lessons for fifth to ninth graders that use picture books to teach about literary elements, including characters, setting, plot, theme, and style.

Teaching emergent readers: collaborative library lesson plans — Sauerteig, Judy. {IL PF, 372.41} — Libraries Unlimited, 2005, 147p

Contains a collection of lesson plans designed for teachers of first and second grade readers, including bibliographic information, with overviews of setting, character, plot, and summary for thirty-five chapter books.

Teaching the essentials of reading with picture books — Sweeney, Alyse. {IL PF, 372.4} — Scholastic, 2004, 96p

Contains fifteen lessons that rely on picture books to introduce students in kindergarten through second grade to the reading skills of phonemic awareness, phonics, fluency, vocabulary, and comprehension.

Teaching with picture books in the middle school — Tiedt, Iris M. {IL PF, 373.133} — International Reading Association, 2000, 221p

Explores the use of picture books in the middle school classroom, and offers teaching suggestions, instructional strategies, and reproducible lesson plans, as well as lists of resources and books.

Teaching writing with picture books as models: lessons and strategies for using the power of picture books to teach the elements of great writing in the upper grades — Kurstedt, Rosanne. {IL PF, 372.62} — Scholastic Professional Books, 2000, 128p

Presents lessons designed to show teachers how to use picture books to teach writing skills to students in grades four through eight, and includes recommended reading lists.

Terrific connections with authors, illustrators, and storytellers: real space and virtual links — Buzzeo, Toni. {IL PF, 372.64} — Libraries Unlimited, 1999, 185p

Explains how teachers can use the Internet to find authors, illustrators, and storytellers that will come visit the students in their classrooms.

To be a boy, to be a reader: engaging teen and preteen boys in active literacy — Brozo, William G. {IL PF, 428.4} — International Reading Association, 2002, 196p

Presents ten positive male archetypes in literature that spark boys' interest in reading, shows how these archetypes can be used in the classroom, and provides a list of over three hundred representative literary works.

Using picture books to teach language arts standards in grades 3-5 — Copeland, Brenda S. {IL PF, 372.133} — Libraries Unlimited, 2006, 158p

A guide to using picture books to help students in grades three through five master language arts skills that includes lists of appropriate titles, reproducible worksheets, writing activities, reading-based activities, and more.

Worth a thousand words: an annotated guide to picture books for older readers — Ammon, Bette DeBruyne. {IL PF, 011.62} — Libraries Unlimited, 1996, 210p

A guide to 645 picture books intended for, or appropriate to use, with readers in fourth grade and above, arranged alphabetically by author or editor's last name, and including title, publisher, illustrator, a synopsis, and suggestions for including each book in the school curriculum.

"You gotta be the book": teaching engaged and reflective reading with adolescents — Wilhelm, Jeffrey D. {IL PF, 428.4} — Teachers College Press, NCTE, 1997, 190p

Utilizes reader-response literary theory, and draws upon studies of truly engaged adolescent readers, to present a theory for teaching reluctant students how to "see" what they read, ensuring their interest and success.

APPENDIX 3

Great Book Sources for All Readers

Educators

Kathleen Baxter—Nonfiction and boy-book expert; author of *Gotcha, Gotcha Again,* and *Gotcha for Boys*; BER consultant for Best Books of the Decade and Books for Boys <http://www.kathleenbaxter.com/>

Esme Raji Codell—teacher, librarian, and author of *Sahara Special* and *How to Get Your Child to Love Reading* <http://planetesme.com/>

Deborah B. Ford—

Scary, Gross, and Enlightening: Books for Boys <http://www.kn.att.com/wired/fil/pages/listboysandau.html>

Some of the Best Books <http://www.kn.att.com/wired/fil/pages/listbestboode.html>

Libraries Matter Blog <http://www.deborahford.blogspot.com/>

Judy Freeman—librarian, storyteller, and author; BER consultant for Best Books of the Decade K-6 and Best Books of the Year K-6 <http://www.judyreadsbooks.com/>

Nancy Keane—librarian and author of many books, including *Booktalking Across the Curriculum: The Middle Years;* BER presenter; Web page contains lists of books garnered from listservs <http://www.nancykeane.com/>

Kathleen Odean—expert on Children's and Young Adult Books
<http://www.kathleenodean.com/>

San Diego City Schools IMC—produces recommended booklists 3 to 4 times annually
<http://www2.sandi.net/IMC/>

Peggy Sharp—known for her presentation of children's books and how to use them; a BER consultant on K-6 Books of the Year
<http://peggysharp.com/>

APPENDIX 4

Reading Interest Survey

1. Are you a
   - ❏ Boy
   - ❏ Girl

2. How many books are in your
   - ❏ Room _____
   - ❏ House _____

3. How do you choose what to read? (Check as many as apply.)
   - ❏ Cover
   - ❏ Length
   - ❏ Author
   - ❏ Illustrator
   - ❏ Series

4. How much do you read before you decide you

   Like it _____

   Don't like it _____

5. I prefer
   - ❏ Paperback
   - ❏ Hardback

6.   I have a public library card.
     ❑ Yes
     ❑ No

7.   Where do you read most?
     ❑ Classroom
     ❑ Bedroom
     ❑ Other room in house _____
     ❑ In a vehicle
     ❑ Other _____

8.   How do you find out about books?
     ❑ Internet _____
     ❑ Friends _____
     ❑ Teachers _____
     ❑ School Library
     ❑ Book Stores
     ❑ Other _____

9.   What kind of books do you like to read? Check all that apply.
     ❑ Adventure
     ❑ Science Fiction
     ❑ Mystery
     ❑ Series
     ❑ Fantasy
     ❑ Fiction
     ❑ Nonfiction (name three subjects)

     _____

     ❑ Biography
     ❑ Sports
     ❑ Magazines (Which ones?)

     _____

- ❑ War
- ❑ History
- ❑ Short Stories
- ❑ Poetry
- ❑ How to do it Books
- ❑ Drawing
- ❑ Humor
- ❑ Newspaper (Which sections?) _____
- ❑ Other _____

10. Do you have a hobby? If so what is it? _____

11. Who read to you when you were younger? _____

    When did they stop? _____

12. How much time do you spend reading
    - ❑ For school work _____
    - ❑ For fun _____

13. Name your 3 favorite authors or illustrators.

    _____

    _____

    _____

14. What are your favorite books? _____

15. What are you reading now? _____

16. If you had money to spend on books for the classroom or school
    library what would you buy? _____

    _____

    _____

17. Complete this sentence. When I finish reading a book, the first thing I want to do is _____.

18. Do you collect anything? _____ What? _____

19. What do you like least about reading?

_____

_____

_____

20. What you do like most about reading?

_____

_____

_____

21. What else would you like to say about reading and books?

_____

_____

_____

Works Cited

Smith, Michael W. *"Reading Don't Fix No Chevys": Literacy in the Lives of Young Men*. Portsmouth, NH: Heinemann, 2002.

Smith, Michael W. *Going with the Flow: How to Engage Boys (and Girls) in Their Literacy Learning*. Portsmouth, NH: Heinemann, 2006.

Wilhelm, Jeffrey D. *"You Gotta Be the Book": Teaching Engaged and Reflective Reading with Adolescents*. New York, NY: Teachers College Press, NCTE, 1997.

Index

A

Abbott, Tony, 56

The absolutely true diary of a part-time Indian, 88

Action strategies for deepening comprehension, 127

Activities, 61-62, 104, 137-40

Adler, David A., 15, 44, 82

Adventure books, 49-62

The adventures of Daniel Boom, a.k.a. Loud Boy. 1, Sound off!, 28

The adventures of the dish and the spoon, 121

Agee, Jon, 67, 93, 125

Ain't nothing but a man, 19

Airman, 51, 88

Akimbo, 118

Alcatraz versus the evil Librarians, 70

Alcatraz versus the Scrivener's Bones, 88

The alchemist, 71

Alex Rider, 119

Alex Rider series, 49, 52, 75, 101, 119

Alexie, Sherman, 88

Alfred Kropp, 120

Alfred Kropp: the seal of Solomon, 51

Alfred Kropp: the thirteenth skull, 52

Alice's adventures in Wonderland, 97

All that remains, 121

Allard, Harry, 102

Allende, Isabel, 98, 122

Almond, David, 101, 124

Alvin Ho, 89

The amazing life of birds, 121

America at war, 81

American born Chinese, 121

The American story, 121

Ammon, Bette DeBruyne, 132

The Amulet of Samarkand, 97

Anderson, M. T., 84, 122

Animals. *See* Natural Science 500s

Ansberry, Karen Rohrich, 130

The ant bully, 98

Antsy does time, 89

Applegate, Katherine, 90

Ark angel, 52

Armstrong, Jennifer, 121

Arnold, Tedd, 65, 117, 124

Aronson, Marc, 4, 7, 85

The arrival, 28

Art. *See* Fine Arts (Arts, Music, Sports) 700s

Artemis Fowl, 119

Artemis Fowl: the graphic novel, 28

Artemis Fowl: the time paradox, 52

Arthur Trilogy, 119

As good as anybody, 6

At Gleason's gym, 15

Attack of the Turtle, 81

Audio books, 108, 111

Avi, 57, 84, 110, 118

Awful Ogre running wild, 17

Awful Ogre's awful day, 121

B

Babbitt, Natalie, 102, 112

Backes, Laura, 127

Bad Bear Detectives, 117

The bad beginning, 98

G

H

Manning, Mick, 9
Marrin, Albert, 124
Martin Bridge, 92, 117
Mary Poppins, 100
Mary Shelley's Frankenstein, 31
Marzollo, Jean, 117
Masoff, Joy, 125
Masterpiece, 92
Matilda, 100
Maximum Ride, 120
McAllister, Margaret, 118
McCaughrean, Geraldine, 125
McDonald, Megan, 94, 117
McEwan, James, 45
McLeod, Bob, 32
Measle and the . . . , 120
Mebus, Scott, 73
Melvin Beederman Superhero, 118
Melvin Beederman Superhero
    series, 67, 118
Menzel, Peter, 15
Mercy Watson, 117
Mexican whiteboy, 92
Michelson, Richard, 6
The mighty 12, 31
Mikaelsen, Ben, 54, 126
Miller, Connie Colwell, 14
Miller, Donna P., 131
Million Dollar, 118
Million Dollar Book series, 43, 118
The million dollar goal, 43
The million dollar putt, 43
The million dollar shot, 43
Millions, 100
The Missing series, 54
Mistmantle Chronicles, 118
Monster Blood Tattoo, 120
Montmorency, 120
More bones, 20
More parts, 124
Morgan, Christopher, 67
Morris, Carla, 110

Morris, Gerald, 120
Mortal engines, 124
Movies, based on books, 97-103
Mr. Chickee's messy mission, 55
Mr. Lincoln's boys, 92
Mrs. Frisby and the rats of NIMH,
    100
Mucci, Michael, 30
Muhammad Ali, 16
Murphy, Jim, 21
Music. *See* Fine Arts (Arts, Music,
    Sports) 700s
My dog may be a genius, 18
My father, the dog, 124
My Weird School, 118
Myers, Walter Dean, 41, 85, 123,
    125
Mysteries of the mummy kids, 7
Mysteries unwrapped, 5
The mysterious Benedict Society, 55
*The mysterious Benedict Society
    and the perilous journey*, 55
The mysterious universe, 11
Mystery and Adventure books,
    49-62
Mystery chart, 60
Mythological creatures, 5

N

Nailed, 124
The name of this book is secret, 55
Nation, 92
Natural Science (Animals, Nature)
    500s, 8-13
Nature. *See* Natural Science
    (Animals, Nature) 500s
Naylor, Phyllis Reynolds, 101
Neandertals, 11
The Neddiad, 56
Nelson, Kadir, 47
Nelson, Scott Reynolds, 19